THE ESSENTIAL
RUTH STONE

THE ESSENTIAL
RUTH STONE

EDITED BY BIANCA STONE

COPPER CANYON PRESS
PORT TOWNSEND, WASHINGTON

Cover photograph courtesy of the Ruth Stone Estate

Painting on p. 65, by Phoebe Stone, appeared in *Who Is the Widow's Muse?*

Copper Canyon Press is in residence at Fort Worden State Park in Port Townsend,
Washington, under the auspices of Centrum. Centrum is a gathering place for artists
and creative thinkers from around the world, students of all ages and backgrounds, and
audiences seeking extraordinary cultural enrichment.

LIBRARY OF CONGRESS CATALOGING-IN-PUBLICATION DATA
Names: Stone, Ruth, author. | Stone, Bianca, editor.
Title: The essential Ruth Stone / edited by Bianca Stone.
Description: Port Townsend, Washington : Copper Canyon Press, [2020]
Includes index. | Summary: "A collection drawn from Ruth Stone's
previous books" — Provided by publisher.
Identifiers: LCCN 2020017913 | ISBN 9781556596087 (paperback)
Subjects: LCGFT: Poetry.
Classification: LCC PS3537.T6817 E87 2020 | DDC 811/.54 — dc23
LC record available at https://lccn.loc.gov/2020017913

98765432 FIRST PRINTING

COPPER CANYON PRESS
Post Office Box 271
Port Townsend, Washington 98368

www.coppercanyonpress.org

Contents

Cheap: New Poems and Ballads (1975)

Second-Hand Coat: Poems New and Selected (1987)

Who Is the Widow's Muse? (1991)

Simplicity (1995)

Ordinary Words (1999)

In the Next Galaxy (2002)

In the Dark (2004)

What Love Comes To: New & Selected Poems (2008)

Editor's Note

Ruth Stone's poems are intuitive, elegant, and intense. In them, she intrudes on the overlooked spaces of the everyday and the existential. "Pleasure me not, for love's pleasure drained me / Deep as an artesian well; / The pitiless blood-letter veined me," she writes in "In the Interstices," the title's definitive word a tiny, prevailing space—the negative space, the in-between. Stone lived for this space (as all great poets do), yet she had a particular gift for seeing it—a wry surgeon examining the bays between organs to discover what disoriented human dread hid there.

It was in that abstract yet casually affirmed interior space that Stone raised her daughters, and they their children in turn. Amid the daily domestic she subtly demanded the creation of art from her daughters, students, and friends who peeked into the interstitial cavities she exposed. And so, like an apprentice following around a blacksmith, I followed my grandmother, muddling devoutly in the interstices of her redheaded lyricism. And while I cannot "shake my grandma out of me"—her language deep in my head—I actually find that I look upon her work with utter unfamiliarity. No matter how many times you read the writing of someone who *really* undoes you, you always find newness there. In compiling this book, I was hit again and again with her refreshing authenticity. To read great poetry is an unfolding that is never finished, and meaning only ripens with time.

Stone's poems are filled with glaring revelations about both the human condition and the natural world. Landscape, animals, insects are all common themes, as often as Greyhound buses and callous strangers. "And each of his bitches knows her own parcel / By the singular smell of her feces," she writes in "Habitat," a calculated and luxuriously adorned poem that stalks the habits of the endangered wolverine, merging plain fact with a nuanced commentary on both the tragic wonder of nature and the ubiquity of patriarchal structures. Stone is expert at texturing the subjective and the political with the natural world, neither detracting from the other. Her poems play with scholarship on her own terms. Science, grammar, pedagogy—she makes fun of culture while also celebrating it. She grieves and laughs in the same gasp, taking sagacious liberties and taking on self-deprecating constraints. And can we ask for more of our poets?

Tragedy ends up defining poets. Early in her life, Stone left her white-collar first husband for her lover — a Jewish immigrant, Harvard poet, fiction writer, and scholar, Walter Stone. Despite their extraordinary and passionate love, poverty and psychological difficulty plagued them. In 1959 — the year after they purchased their first house in Goshen, Vermont (then with three daughters in tow), and the year Ruth's first book of poetry, *In an Iridescent Time*, was published — Walter Stone very suddenly committed suicide. This traumatic loss affixed to Stone's identity as a poet forever after, as did her house in Vermont, which became a refuge and sanctuary for the family's unpredictable life.

In 1971, Harcourt Brace Jovanovich published her second book, *Topography and Other Poems*, after which she began publishing more steadily. Ruth's unique voice, championed reading style, and bohemian personality (akin to Lucille Ball meets Edna St. Vincent Millay) brought her a cult following. It wasn't until the late 1990s that higher honors and awards drew national attention to her. But macular degeneration, the second great tragedy of her life, was already descending, impairing her ability to write, read, and teach.

Stone's sensual confidence and strong personality were simultaneously symbolic of and at odds with her era. "I am amorphous with all deflowered brides," she writes as "In the Interstices" nears its end. Physicality and intellect converging, Ruth had to deal with the great cultural resistance toward female poets' sexuality. Intellectual, creative, self-possessed women have always been dismissed. It is a trend only now being undone. But like other women poets of the time (Bernadette Mayer, Sharon Olds, Lucille Clifton, and many others), she persisted in her unique, genius way.

Stone's late poems pare down the metrical density of her early work and steer toward more directness in her philosophical foundations. Ruth's poems are not so much about the disjointedness of breath as they are about the roar and rank of direct words; tone and bombast of thought; the smack of a rhyme as it launches us unexpectedly but skillfully into the simple golden precision of her lines. "Wanting and dissatisfaction / are the main ingredients / of happiness," she writes in "Wanting," a poem that characterizes her humor toward the hedonistic yearning in human nature. Her poetry constructs a whole experience, from the academic dissent of her early work to the sardonic sagacity of the later period.

In a way, it was easy for me to pare down to the essential poems of Ruth Stone, with help from friends and family. But what I also looked for in editing this volume, perhaps, were the unsung pieces that illustrate her vital brilliance as a poet. It's easy for an author to get bogged down by a characterization made during her most publicized times — what becomes all that the public knows of her abilities, without fully grasping the intricacies of the poet's oeuvre. What we must do is investigate writers further, go deeper after they are gone — as in recent studies of Emily Dickinson's biographical mythologies. My hope with *The Essential Ruth Stone* is that new readers and those already familiar with her poems will glean fresh insights and make discoveries. It is a testament to the greatness of a writer that we can continue to examine, with curiosity and openness, indefinitely, the merits of her work.

*

I would like to thank Ruth Stone's daughters for their profound devotion to their mother's legacy: Marcia Croll, Phoebe Stone, and Abigail Stone. Also the grandchildren who helped pick these poems: Walter Stone, Hillery Stone, and Nora Swan Croll. Thank you to Ben Pease for his tireless work on the Ruth Stone House mission. Thank you to Chard deNiord for his input on what was and is "essential" and for his dogged commitment to Ruth. And most of all, thank you to Grandma. I hope this makes you proud. You were essential to all of us.

Bianca Stone
Brandon, Vermont

THE ESSENTIAL
RUTH STONE

In an Iridescent Time

1959

Snow

Plentiful snow deepens the path to the woods.
Jay, hawing, shakes the juniper,
Gray squirrel and titmouse trick in hectic moods,
Fluff buffeters of down and fur.
Jay skates on ice-blue air with bluer flight,
Dives in down-soft whirl and comes up light.
The dried and dead hackberry dangles white,
Tall trees droop down while ground grows up,
And the powder-white snuff blows from the wind's lip,
Sneezing the world; still the old lady shakes her puff
In the well of the wind, and feathers fly from the rip.

The Magnet

I loved my lord, my black-haired lord, my young love
Thin faced, pointed like a fox,
And he, singing and sighing, with the bawdy went crying
Up the hounds, through thicket he leaped, through bramble,
And crossed the river on rocks.
And there alongside the sheep and among the ewes and lambs,
With terrible sleep he cunningly laid his hoax.

Ah fey, and ill-gotten, and wicked his tender heart,
Even as they with their bahs and their niggles, rumped up the thistle
    and bit
With their delicate teeth the flowers and the seeds and the leaf,
He leaped with a cry as coarse as the herders, "Come, I will start,
Come now, my pretties, and dance to the hunting horn and the slit
Of your throbbing throats, and make me a coat out of grief."
And they danced, he was fey, and they danced, and the coat they made
Turned all of an innocent mind, and a single love, into beasts afraid.

Was it I called him back? was it hunger? was it the world?
Not my tears, not those cries of the murdered, but 'twas the fox
Hid in the woods who called, and the smell of the fox, burned in
    his mind,
The fox in his den, smiling, around his red body his fine plume curled,
Out of the valley and across the river, leaving his sheep's hair, he left
    the maligned flocks,
I heard him coming through brambles, through narrow forests, I bid my
    nights unwind,
I bid my days turn back, I broke my windows, I unsealed my locks.

In an Iridescent Time

My mother, when young, scrubbed laundry in a tub,
She and her sisters on an old brick walk
Under the apple trees, sweet rub-a-dub.
The bees came round their heads, the wrens made talk.
Four young ladies each with a rainbow board
Honed their knuckles, wrung their wrists to red,
Tossed back their braids and wiped their aprons wet.
The Jersey calf beyond the back fence roared;
And all the soft day, swarms about their pet
Buzzed at his big brown eyes and bullish head.
Four times they rinsed, they said. Some things they starched,
Then shook them from the baskets two by two,
And pinned the fluttering intimacies of life
Between the lilac bushes and the yew:
Brown gingham, pink, and skirts of Alice blue.

Speculation

In the coolness here I care
Not for the down-pressed noises overhead,
I hear in my pearly bone the wear
Of marble under the rain; nothing is truly dead,
There is only the wearing away,
The changing of means. Nor eyes I have
To tell how in the summer the mourning dove
Rocks on the hemlock's arm, nor ears to rend
The sad regretful mind
With the call of the horned lark.
I lie so still that the earth around me
Shakes with the weight of day;
I do not mind if the vase
Holds decomposed cut flowers, or if they send
One of their kind to tidy up. Such play
I have no memories of,
Nor of the fire-bush flowers, or the bark
Of the rough pine where the crows
With their great haw and flap
Circle in kinned excitement when a wind blows.
I am kin with none of these,
Nor even wed to the yellowing silk that splits;
My sensitive bones, which dreaded,
As all the living do, the dead,
Wait for some unappointed pattern. The wits
Of countless centuries dry in my skull and overhead
I do not heed the first rain out of winter,
Nor do I care what they have planted. At my center
The bone glistens; of wondrous bones I am made;
And alone shine in a phosphorous glow,
So, in this little plot where I am laid.

The Season

I know what calls the Devil from the pits,
With a thief's fingers there he slouches and sits;
I've seen him passing on a frenzied mare,
Bitter eyed on her haunches out to stare;
He rides her cruel and he rides her easy.
Come along spring, come along sun, come along field daisy.

Smell the foxy babies, smell the hunting dog;
The shes have whelped, the cocks and hens have lost their wits;
And cry, "Why," cry the spring peepers, "Why," each little frog.
He rides her cruel and he rides her easy;
Come along spring, come along sun, come along field daisy.

In the Interstices

Pleasure me not, for love's pleasure drained me
Deep as an artesian well;
The pitiless blood-letter veined me.
Long grew the parasite before its fill.
Lover, smile the other way, nor ply me with evil
Who am surfeited and taste the shadows of gray;
Nor sway me with promises to rouse my thirst
And fill me with that passion beyond lust;
Nor romp my body in the wake of the mind's play.

How tired, how enervated, how becalmed I am.
That island toward which I strove in my salt tides
Has drifted out beyond the listless swell and formed
A hostile continent. I am amorphous with all deflowered brides,
Who, with their floodgates sundered, drowned when they were stormed.

Orchard

The mare roamed soft about the slope,
Her rump was like a dancing girl's.
Gentle beneath the apple trees
She pulled the grass and shook the flies.
Her forelocks hung in tawny curls;
She had a woman's limpid eyes,
A woman's patient stare that grieves.
And when she moved among the trees,
The dappled trees, her look was shy,
She hid her nakedness in leaves.
A delicate though weighted dance
She stepped while flocks of finches flew
From tree to tree and shot the leaves
With songs of golden twittering;
How admirable her tender stance.
And then the apple trees were new,
And she was new, and we were new,
And in the barns the stallions stamped
And shook the hills with trumpeting.

The Splinter

I had a little silver manikin
Who walked and talked and petted me;
I pampered him, he pampered me; we
Were convivial. On the gray streets
Of many a gray city he wept with me.
Oh then how miniature was sin,
How clear its purpose like a looking glass
To show me my young girl's skin.

But I looked and looked again
And saw a blue cadaverous vein.
I will grow old, I cried,
You are a silver groom,
I will be a brown leather bride.
You are imperishable, still by my side
You will shine in the wine
That puckers my hide.

And in those sad reflections
I took a silver hammer made of words,
And hit him and he shattered like bright birds
Flying in all directions.
All night and all eternity I cried,
And in the morning by the gray light
I found his splinter in my side,
And when I drew it out, I saw it was glass —
The finest concave mirror, silver white
And backed with brightest silver. Oh alas,
He was a manikin of glass with all his light turned in,
And mirrored in the dark, the manikin.

Topography and Other Poems

1971

The Talking Fish

My love's eyes are red as the sargasso
With lights behind the iris like a cephalopod's.
The weeds move slowly, November's diatoms
Stain the soft stagnant belly of the sea.
Mountains, atolls, coral reefs,
Do you desire me? Am I among the jellyfish of your griefs?
I comb my sorrows singing; any doomed sailor can hear
The rising and falling bell and begin to wish
For home. There is no choice among the voices
Of love. Even a carp sings.

Being Human,

Though all the force to hold the parts together
And service love reversed, turned negative,
Fountained in self-destroying flames
And rained ash in volcanic weather;
We are still here where you left us
With our own kind: unstable strangers
Trembling in the sound waves of meaningless
Eloquence. They say we live.
They say, as they rise on the horizon
And come toward us dividing and dividing,
That we must save; that we must solve; transcend
Cohesive and repelling flesh, protoplasm, particles, and survive.
I do not doubt we will; I do not doubt all things are possible,
Even that wildest hope that we may meet beyond the grave.

Tenacity

Can it be over so soon?
Why, only a day or so ago
You let me win at chess
While you felt my dress
Around the knees.
That room we went to
Sixty miles away —
Have those bus trips ended?
The willows turning by,
Drooping like patient beasts
Under their yellow hair
On the winter fields;
Crossing the snow streams —
Was it for the last time?
Going to meet you, I thought
I saw the embalmer standing there
On the ordinary dirty street
Of that gross and ordinary city
Which opened like a paper flower
At the ballet, at the art gallery,
In those dark booths drinking beer.
One night leaning in a stone doorway
I waited for the wrong person,
And when he came I noticed the dead
Blue color of his skin under the neon light,
And the odor of rubbish behind a subway shed.
I sit for hours at the window
Preparing a letter; you are coming toward me,
We are balanced like dancers in memory,
I feel your coat, I smell your clothes,
Your tobacco; you almost touch me.

The Excuse

Do they write poems when they have something to say,
Something to think about,
Rubbed from the world's hard rubbing in the excess of every day?
The summer I was twenty-four in San Francisco. You and I.
The whole summer seemed like a cable-car ride over the gold bay.
But once in a bistro, angry at one another,
We quarreled about a taxi fare. I doubt
That it was the fare we quarreled about,
But one excuse is as good as another
In the excess of passion, in the need to be worn away.

Do they know it is cleanness of skin, firmness of flesh that matters?
It is so difficult to look at the deprived, or smell their decay.
But now I am among them. I, too, am a leper, a warning.
I hold out my crippled fingers; my voice flatters
Everyone who comes this way. In the weeds of mourning,
Groaning and gnashing, I display
Myself in malodorous comic wrappings and tatters,
In the excess of passion, in the need to be worn away.

The Plan

I said to myself, do you have a plan?
And the answer was always, no, I have no plan.
Then I would say to myself, you must think of one.
But what happened went on, chaotic with necessary pain.
During the winter the dogs dug moles from their runs
And rolled them blind on the frozen road.
Then the crossbills left at the equinox.
All this time I tried to think of a plan,
Something to bring the points together.
I saw that we move in a circle
But I was wordless in the field.
The smell of green steamed, everything shoved,
But I folded my hands and sat on the rocks.
Here I am, I said, with my eyes.
When they have fallen like marbles from their sockets,
What will become of this? And then I remembered
That there were young moles in my mind's eye,
Whose pink bellies shaded to mauve plush,
Whose little dead snouts sparkled with crystals of frost;
And it came to me, the blind will be leading the blind.

Poles

In the summer under the light ease of laundry fluttering
In the air along with our portion of birds, insects and lifting leaves,
The simple truth is I confine your picture to one room
Where occasionally I go to be struck again by its fierce tragic stare.
Summoned to it by a world of trifles, in what I know is a mockery
Of despair; it depresses me. Though you cannot condemn or pardon
My being one with blood and oxygen, I damn myself
For having eyes and ears and wits, all the time I stand before you
Shaking my head at the shame of anything that lies down and dies.

Green Apples

In August we carried the old horsehair mattress
To the back porch
And slept with our children in a row.
The wind came up the mountain into the orchard
Telling me something;
Saying something urgent.
I was happy.
The green apples fell on the sloping roof
And rattled down.
The wind was shaking me all night long;
Shaking me in my sleep
Like a definition of love,
Saying, this is the moment,
Here, now.

Habitat

The wolverine, whose numbers remain somewhat constant,
Lays claim to upwards of half a million acres
As his own and his few bitches'.
A relative of the glutton; lonely patriarch;
Restless, cautious and suspicious of man.
(The mammalogist Adolph Murie says
That during his study of the mammals of Mt. Rainier,
He never saw a wolverine.)
He is a shy animal and keeps to outsized, secret paths.
He is the largest of the mustelines —
That sub-family which claims the mink, the weasel.
Dr. Krott is amazed at the uniformity of the species,
Which is of circumpolar distribution,
Inhabiting the vast coniferous forests of the north.
The quality of the pelts in Manchuria, however,
Is said to be slightly inferior.
Man has driven him from the southern fringes
Of Latvia, Estonia, and some Russian provinces.
His body averages three feet long including his tail.
His weight is sometimes nearly eighty pounds.
He is built for endurance;
Indeed, it is said that lumbosacrally he is overbuilt.
When engaged with a wolf in the powdery snow of the wooded area,
The wolverine happily proves to be superior.
Since man has rid himself of the plague of wolves,
The wolverine is moving into the tundra.
He is an animal fond of play and can learn something new
To his innate modes of behavior. When caught in a trap
He may bite off the tortured limb and escape.
He runs in serpentine lines with frequent change of direction.
Strong hunger keeps a wolverine awake.
In winter he is the scourge of the Laplanders' reindeer
His normal gait is the gallop, and when pursued
He can cover forty miles without a rest.
Though carnivorous, he decimates at the proper season

The larvae of wasps. He is a voracious rampant eater of wasp larvae,
Digging them out in the singing buzz and sting
From their mud-packed nitches.
He has a fur much valued by northern peoples,
Which does not mat; men wear it about their faces.
He marks off his half-million acres with his own urine,
And each of his bitches knows her own parcel
By the singular smell of her feces.

Fairy Tales

The ugly duckling...
I stood behind my father's chair so he couldn't see my tears
When he read it to me. Hans Andersen,
I rise from your feathers every spring
And shake the snow out of my windows. The sulphur sears
My eyes in a world of match girls' luminous poverty.
I hear your hosannas that life is real and cruel.
The mad stream that takes the brave tin soldier down the flood
Flows by here. While he passes, impractical child,
On his way to death in this strange dream;
Is he still seeing the beautiful, the good?

Advice

My hazard wouldn't be yours, not ever;
But every doom, like a hazelnut, comes down
To its own worm. So I am rocking here
Like any granny with her apron over her head
Saying, lordy me. It's my trouble.
There's nothing to be learned this way.
If I heard a girl crying help
I would go to save her;
But you hardly ever hear those words.
Dear children, you must try to say
Something when you are in need.
Don't confuse hunger with greed;
And don't wait until you are dead.

Seat Belt Fastened?

Old Bill Pheasant won't trim his beard.
Weep, my daughters, and have you heard?
Sing, little otters; don't be afraid.
There's a rustle in the oak leaves
Down by the river. Oh, the moving mirror
And the hearer and the word.

Old Bill wandered in my waking dream,
A river dream; when I saw him come
I was riding by with my gas tank high
Down to Otter Creek from my just-right home.
And he put his beard in the window and said,
"It's sleazy and greasy but it's in your head.
Tell me, woman, do you carry a comb?"
Too far from home to the river, I shammed.
"Better not come this far," I said.
But old Bill Pheasant said he'd be damned.
And we backfired down. Oh, daughters, do you tread
On the leaf fall, fern all—picked and pocketed?

Now tell me when we're passing, and tell me when we gain.
And laugh, little children, while our gas tank's high.
"Give thanks for desire," was all he said.
"It'll either clear up or snow or rain."
So we tweaked his beard and we punched his head.
Is your seat belt fastened? Do you sleep in your bed?
If you're stuck in the river can you shift to red?
If you're coming are you going?
If you're living are you dead?

And we drove him away where the otters play,
Where it's twice on Sunday in the regular way,
Where they say what they know and they know what they say,
And the good time's coming on yesterday.

Metamorphosis

Now that I am old, all I want to do is try;
But when I was young, if it wasn't easy I let it lie,
Learning through my pores instead,
And it did neither of us any good.

For now she is gone who slept away my life,
And I am ignorant who inherited,
Though the head has grown so lively that I laugh,
"Come look, come stomp, come listen to the drum."

I see more now than then; but she who had my eyes
Closed them in happiness, and wrapped the dark
In her arms and stole my life away,
Singing in dreams of what was sure to come.

I see it perfectly, except the beast
Fumbles and falters, until the others wince.
Everything shimmers and glitters and shakes with unbearable longing,
The dancers who cannot sleep, and the sleepers who cannot dance.

Wild Asters

I am here to worship the blue
asters along the brook;
not to carry pollen on my legs,
or rub strutted wings
in mindless sucking;
but to feel with my eyes
the loss of you and me,
not in the powdered mildew
that spreads from leaf to leaf,
but in the glorious absence of grief
to see what was not meant to be seen,
the clusters, the aggregate, the undenying multiplicity.

Topography

Do I dare to think that I alone am
The sum total of every night hand searching in the
Pounding pounding over the universe of veins, sweat,
Dust in the sheets with noses that got in the way?
Yes, I remember the turning and holding,
The heavy geography; but map me again, Columbus.

Cheap: New Poems and Ballads

1975

Bargain

I was not ready for this world
Nor will I ever be.
But came an infant periled
By my mother sea,
And crying piteously.

Before my father's sword,
His heavy voice of thunder,
His cloud hung fiery eyes,
I ran, a living blunder.

After the hawker's cries,
Desiring to be shared
I hid among the flies.

Myself became the fruit and vendor.
I began to sing.
Mocking the caged birds
I made my offering.

"Sweet cream and curds...
Who will have me,
Who will have me?"
And close upon my words,
"I will," said poverty.

Codicil

I am still bitter about the last place we stayed.
The bed was really too small for both of us.
In that same rooming house
Walls were lined with filing cases,
Drawers of birds' eggs packed in cotton.
The landlady described them.
As widow of the ornithologist,
Actually he was a postal clerk,
She was proprietor of the remains.
Had accompanied him on his holidays
Collecting eggs. Yes,
He would send her up the tree
And when she faltered he would shout,
"Put it in your mouth. Put it in your mouth."
It was nasty, she said,
Closing a drawer with her knee.
Faintly blue, freckled, mauve, taupe,
Chalk white eggs.
As we turned the second flight of stairs
Toward a mattress unfit for two,
Her voice would echo up the well,
Something about an electric kettle
At the foot of our bed.
Eggs, eggs, eggs in secret muted shapes in my head;
Hundreds of unborn wizened eggs.
I think about them when I think of you.

The Tree

I was a child when you married me,
A child I was when I married you.
But I was a regular Midwest child,
And you were a Jew.

My mother needled my father cold,
My father gambled his weekly gold,
And I stayed young in my mind, though old,
As your regular children do.

I didn't rah and I hardly raved.
I loved my pa while my mother slaved,
And it rubbed me raw how she scrimped and saved
When I was so new.

Then you took me in with your bony knees,
And it wasn't them that I wanted to please—
It was Jesus Christ that I had to squeeze;
Oh, glorious you.

Life in the dead sprang up in me,
I walked the waves of the salty sea,
I wept for my mother in Galilee,
My ardent Jew.

Love and touch and unity.
Parting and joining; the trinity
Was flesh, the mind and the will to be.
The world grew through me like a tree.

Flesh was the citadel but Rome
Was right as rain. From my humble home
I walked to the scaffold of pain, and the dome
Of heaven wept for her sensual son
Whom the Romans slew.

Was it I who was old when you hung, my Jew?
I shuffled and snuffled and whined for you.
And the child climbed up where the dead tree grew
And slowly died while she wept for you.

The goyim wept for the beautiful Jew.

Habit

Every day I dig you up
And wipe off the rime
And look at you.
You are my joke,
My poem.
Your eyelids pull back from their sockets.
Your mouth mildews in scallops.
Worm filaments sprout from the pockets
Of your good suit.
I hold your sleeves in my arms;
Your waist drops a little putrid flesh.
I show you my old shy breasts.

Being a Woman

You can talk to yourself all you want to.
After all, you were the only one who ever heard
What you were saying. And even you forgot
Those brilliant flashes seen from afar, like Toledo
Brooding, burning up from the Moorish scimitar.

Sunk in umber, illuminated at the edges by fitful lightning,
You subside in the suburbs. Hidden in the shadow of hedges
You urge your dog to lift his leg on the neighbor's shrubs.

Soldiers are approaching. They are everywhere.
Behind the lamp-post the dog sends unknown messages
To the unknown. A sensible union of the senses.
The disengaged ego making its own patterns.
The voice of the urine saying this has washed away my salt,
My minerals. My kidneys bless you, defy you, invite you
To come out and yip with me in the schizophrenic night.

The Nose

Everyone complains about the nose.
If you notice, it is stuck to your face.
In the morning it will be red.
If you are a woman you can cover it with makeup.
If you are a man it means you had a good time last night.
Noses are phallic symbols.
So are fingers, monuments, trees, and cucumbers.
The familiar, "He knows his stuff," should be looked into.
This may be where the word "throes" originated.
There is big business in nose jobs,
The small nose having gained popularity during the Christian boom.
Noses get out of joint but a broken nose
Is never the same thing as a broken heart.
They say, "Bless your heart." "Shake hands." "Blow your nose."
When kissing there is apt to be a battle of wills
Over which side your nose will go on.
While a nosebleed, next to a good cry, is a natural physic;
A nosey person smells you out and looking down your nose
Will make you cross-eyed.
Although the nose is no longer used for rooting and shoving,
It still gets into some unlikely places.
The old sayings: He won by a nose, and,
He cut off his nose to spite his face,
Illustrate the value of the nose.
In conclusion, three out of four children
Are still equipped with noses at birth;
And the nose, more often than not,
Accompanies the body to its last resting place.

Wavering

What makes you think you're so different?
That was my weaker self hanging around outside the door.
The voices over the telephone were accusing, too.
"Must you always be you?" (They had the advantage,
More bold without faces. They swirled a few ice cubes
With a suggestive pause.) For a moment
I took my heart out and held it in my hands.
Then I put it back. This is how it is in a competitive world.
But, I will not eat my own heart. I will not.

The Song of the Absinthe Granny

Among some hills there dwelt in parody
A young woman; me.
I was that gone with child
That before I knew it I had three
And they hung whining and twisting.
Why I wasn't more than thirty-nine
And sparse as a runt fruit tree.
Three pips that plagued the life out of me.
Ah me. It wore me down,
The grubs, the grubbing.
We were two inches thick in dust
For lack of scrubbing.
Diapers and panty-shirts and yolk of eggs.
One day in the mirror I saw my stringy legs
And I looked around
And saw string on the floor,
And string on the chair
And heads like wasps' nests
Full of stringy hair.
"Well," I said, "if you have string, knit.
Knit something, don't just sit."
We had the orchard drops,
But they didn't keep.
The milk came in bottles.
It came until the bottles were that deep
We fell over the bottles.
The milk dried on the floor.
"Drink it up," cried their papa,
And they all began to roar, "More!"
Well, time went on,
Not a bone that wasn't frayed.
Every chit was knicked and bit,
And nothing was paid.
We had the dog spayed.
"It looks like a lifetime,"

Their papa said.
"It's a good life, it's a good wife,
It's a good bed."
So I got the rifle out
To shoot him through the head.
But he went on smiling and sitting
And I looked around for a piece of string
To do some knitting.
Then I picked at the tiling
And the house fell down.
"Now you've done it," he said.
"I'm going to town.
Get them up out of there,
Put them to bed."
"I'm afraid to look," I whimpered,
"They might be dead."
"We're here, Mama, under the shed."
Well, the winters wore on.
We had cats that hung around.
When I fed them they scratched.
How the little nippers loved them.
Cats and brats.
I couldn't see for my head was thatched
But they kept coming in when the door unlatched.
"I'll shave my head," I promised,
"I'll clip my mop.
This caterwauling has got to stop."
Well, all that's finished,
It's all been done.
Those were high kick summers,
It was bald galled fun.
Now the daft time's over
And the string is spun.
I'm all alone
To cull and be furry.
Not an extra page in the spanking story.
The wet britches dried

And the teeth came in.
The last one cried
And no new began.
Those were long hot summers,
Now the sun won't tarry.
My birds have flocked,
And I'm old and wary.
I'm old and worn and a cunning sipper,
And I'll outlive every little nipper.
And with what's left I'm chary,
And with what's left I'm chary.

Second-Hand Coat: Poems New and Selected

1987

Second-Hand Coat

I feel
in her pockets; she wore nice cotton gloves,
kept a handkerchief box, washed her undies,
ate at the Holiday Inn, had a basement freezer,
belonged to a bridge club.
I think when I wake in the morning
that I have turned into her.
She hangs in the hall downstairs,
a shadow with pulled threads.
I slip her over my arms, skin of a matron.
Where are you? I say to myself, to the orphaned body,
and her coat says,
Get your purse, have you got your keys?

Where I Came From

My father put me in my mother
but he didn't pick me out.
I am my own quick woman.
What drew him to my mother?
Beating his drumsticks
he thought — why not?
And he gave her an umbrella.
Their marriage was like that.
She hid ironically in her apron.
Sometimes she cried into the biscuit dough.
When she wanted to make a point
she would sing a hymn or an old song.
He was loose-footed. He couldn't be counted on
until his pockets were empty.
When he was home the kettle drums,
the snare drum, the celeste,
the triangle throbbed.
While he changed their heads,
the drum skins soaked in the bathtub.
Collapsed and wrinkled, they floated
like huge used condoms.

How to Catch Aunt Harriette

Mary Cassatt has her in a striped dress with a
child on her lap, the child's foot in a wash basin.
Or Charlotte Mew speaks in her voice of the feeling
that comes at evening with home-cawing rooks.
Or Aunt Harriette sometimes makes an ineffable
gesture between the lines of Trollope.
In Indianapolis, together we rode the belching city bus to
high school. It was my first year, she was a senior. We were
nauseated every day by the fumes, by the unbearable
streets. Aunt Harriette was the last issue of my
Victorian grandparents. Once after school she
invited me to go with her to Verner's.
What was *Verner's*? I didn't ask and Aunt Harriette didn't say.
We walked three miles down manicured Meridian.
My heels rubbed to soft blisters. Entering an empty
wood-echoing room fronting the sidewalk,
we sat at a plain plank table and Aunt Harriette
ordered two glasses of iced ginger ale.
The varnish of light on Aunt Harriette
had the quality of a small eighteenth-century
Dutch painting. My tongue with all its buds intact
slipped in the amber sting. It was my first hint
of the connoisseur, an induction rarely repeated;
yet so bizarre, so beyond me,
that I planned my entire life from its indications.

Pokeberries

I started out in the Virginia mountains
with my grandma's pansy bed
and my aunt Maud's dandelion wine.
We lived on greens and back-fat and biscuits.
My aunt Maud scrubbed right through the linoleum.
My daddy was a northerner who played drums
and chewed tobacco and gambled.
He married my mama on the rebound.
Who would want an ignorant hill girl with red hair?
They took a Pullman up to Indianapolis
and someone stole my daddy's wallet.
My whole life has been stained with pokeberries.
No man seemed right for me. I was awkward
until I found a good wood-burning stove.
There is no use asking what it means.
With my first piece of ready cash I bought my own
place in Vermont; kerosene lamps, dirt road.
I'm sticking here like a porcupine up a tree.
Like the one our neighbor shot. Its bones and skin
hung there for three years in the orchard.
No amount of knowledge can shake my grandma out of me;
or my aunt Maud; or my mama, who didn't just bite an apple
with her big white teeth. She split it in two.

Curtains

Putting up new curtains,
other windows intrude.
As though it is that first winter in Cambridge
when you and I had just moved in.
Now cold borscht alone in a bare kitchen.

What does it mean if I say this years later?

Listen, last night
I am on a crying jag
with my landlord, Mr. Tempesta.
I sneaked in two cats.
He screams, "No pets! No pets!"
I become my aunt Virginia,
proud but weak in the head.
I remember Anna Magnani.
I throw a few books. I shout.
He wipes his eyes and opens his hands.
OK OK keep the dirty animals
but no nails in the walls.
We cry together.
I am so nervous, he says.

I want to dig you up and say, look,
it's like the time, remember,
when I ran into our living room naked
to get rid of that fire inspector.

See what you miss by being dead?

Winter

The ten o'clock train to New York,
coaches like loaves of bread powdered with snow.
Steam wheezes between the couplings.
Stripped to plywood, the station's cement standing room
imitates a Russian novel. It is now that I remember you.
Your profile becomes the carved handle of a letter knife.
Your heavy-lidded eyes slip under the seal of my widowhood.
It is another raw winter. Stray cats are suffering.
Starlings crowd the edges of chimneys.
It is a drab misery that urges me to remember you.
I think about the subjugation of women and horses;
brutal exposure; weather that forces, that strips.
In our time we met in ornate stations
arching up with nineteenth-century optimism.
I remember you running beside the train waving good-bye.
I can produce a facsimile of you standing
behind a column of polished oak to surprise me.
Am I going toward you or away from you on this train?
Discarded junk of other minds is strewn beside the tracks:
mounds of rusting wire, grotesque pop art of dead motors,
senile warehouses. The train passes a station;
fresh people standing on the platform,
their faces expecting something.
I feel their entire histories ravish me.

Names

My grandmother's name was Nora Swan.
Old Aden Swan was her father. But who was her mother?
I don't know my great-grandmother's name.
I don't know how many children she bore.
Like rings of a tree the years of woman's fertility.
Who were my great-aunt Swans?
For every year a child; diphtheria, dropsy, typhoid.
Who can bother naming all those women churning butter,
leaning on scrub boards, holding to iron bedposts
sweating in labor? My grandmother knew the names
of all the plants on the mountain. Those were the names
she spoke of to me. Sorrel, lamb's ear, spleenwort, heal-all;
never go hungry, she said, when you can gather a pot of greens.
She had a finely drawn head under a smooth cap of hair
pulled back to a bun. Her deep-set eyes were quick to notice
in love and anger. Who are the women who nurtured her for me?
Who handed her in swaddling flannel to my great-grandmother's breast?
Who are the women who brought my great-grandmother tea
and straightened her bed? As anemone in midsummer, the air
cannot find them and Grandmother's been at rest for forty years.
In me are all the names I can remember — pennyroyal, boneset,
bedstraw, toadflax — from whom I did descend in perpetuity.

American Milk

Then the butter we put on our white bread
was colored with butter yellow, a cancerous dye,
and all the fourth grades were taken by streetcar
to the Dunky Company to see milk processed; milk bottles
riding on narrow metal cogs through little doors that flapped.
The sour damp smell of milky-wet cement floors:
we looked through great glass windows at the milk.
Before we were herded back to the streetcar line,
we were each given a half pint of milk in tiny
milk bottles with straws to suck it up. In this way
we gradually learned about our country.

How Aunt Maud Took to Being a Woman

A long hill sloped down to Aunt Maud's brick house.
You could climb an open stairway up the back
to a plank landing where she kept her crocks of wine.
I got sick on stolen angelfood cake and green wine
and slept in her feather bed for a week.
Nobody said a word. Aunt Maud just shifted
the bottles. Aunt's closets were all cedar lined.
She used the same pattern for her housedresses —
thirty years. Plain ugly, closets full of them,
you could generally find a new one cut and laid
out on her sewing machine. She preserved,
she canned. Her jars climbed the basement walls.
She was a vengeful housekeeper. She kept the blinds
pulled down in the parlor. Nobody really walked
on her hardwood floors. You lived in the kitchen.
Uncle Cal spent a lot of time on the back porch
waiting to be let in.

Comments of the Mild

The cabinet squats trembling on its carved legs,
an essence of trappings. Inside on the awkward shelves,
a cast-off bedspread, two stolen books.
From no period at all; in fact, the back legs are not carved,
while the front ones have turned balls. It tries to be Spanish,
Louis Quinze, Sheraton, Hilton Plaza. It is a bastard
from a tract house. There was no cabinetmaker.
It grew with a lot who were cut on band saws,
glued together on an assembly line, and stained
in a warehouse. "I am furniture," it says, in a subdued voice.
Not useful, not even ornamental, it has a certain bulk presence.
It takes the place of those who are not with you.
When you wake in the night, you sense that you are not alone.
There is someone else. But you forget who it is.
Sometimes passing the cabinet, you open the part that looks
like the confessional box. It is stern and empty.
Nothing fits in there, not even your head.

Turn Your Eyes Away

The gendarme came
to tell me you had hung yourself
on the door of a rented room
like an overcoat
like a bathrobe
hung from a hook;
when they forced the door open
your feet pushed against the floor.
Inside your skull
there was no room for us,
your circuits forgot me.
Even in Paris where we never were
I wait for you
knowing you will not come.
I remember your eyes as if I were
someone you had never seen,
a slight frown between your brows
considering me.
How could I have guessed
the plainspoken stranger in your face,
your body, tagged in a drawer,
attached to nothing, incurious.
My sister, my spouse, you said,
in a place on the other side of the earth
where we lay in a single bed
unable to pull apart
breathing into each other,
the Gideon Bible open to the Song of Songs,
the rush of the El train
jarring the window.
As if needles were stuck
in the pleasure zones of our brains,
we repeated everything
over and over and over.

Some Things You'll Need to Know Before You Join the Union

I
At the poetry factory
body poems are writhing and bleeding.
An angry mob of women
is lined up at the back door
hoping for jobs.
Today at the poetry factory
they are driving needles through the poems.
Everyone's excited.
Mr. Po-Biz himself comes in from the front office.
He clenches his teeth.
"Anymore wildcat aborting out there," he hisses,
"and you're all blacklisted."
The mob jeers.

II
The antiwar and human rights poems
are processed in the white room.
Everyone in there wears sterile gauze.
These poems go for a lot.
No one wants to mess up.
There's expensive equipment involved,
The workers have to be heavy,
very heavy.
These poems are packaged in cement.
You frequently hear them drop with a dull thud.

III
Poems are being shipped out
by freight car.
Headed up the ramp
they can't turn back.
They push each other along.
They will go to the packing houses.
The slaughter will be terrible,

an inevitable end of overproduction,
the poetry factory's GNP.
Their shelf life will be brief.

IV

They're stuffing at the poetry factory today.
They're jamming in images
saturated with *as* and *like.*
Lines are being stuffed to their limits.
If a line by chance explodes,
there's a great cheer.
However, most of them don't explode.
Most of them lie down and groan.

V

In the poetry factory
it's very hot.
The bellows are going,
the pressure is building up.
Young poems are being rolled out
ready to be cut.
Whistles are blowing.
Jive is rocking.
Barrels of thin words line the walls.
Fat words like links of sausages
hang on belts.
Floor walkers and straw bosses
take a coffee break.
Only the nervous apprentice
is anywhere near the machines
when a large poem
seems about to come off the assembly line.
"This is it," the apprentice shouts.
"Get my promotion ready!
APR, the quarterlies,
a chapbook, NEA,
a creative writing chair,

the poetry circuit, Yaddo!"
Inside the ambulance
as it drives away
he is still shouting,
"I'll grow a beard,
become an alcoholic,
consider suicide."

Translations

Forty-five years ago, Alexander Mehielovitch Touritzen,
son of a White Russian owner of a silk stocking factory
in Constantinople, we rumpled your rooming-house bed,
sneaked past your landlady and turned your plaster Madonna
to the wall. Are you out there, short vulgar civil-engineer?
Did you know I left you for a Princeton geologist who called me
girlie? Ten years later he was still in the Midwest when he died
under a rock fall. I told you I was pregnant. You gave me money
for the abortion. I lied to you. I needed clothes to go out with
the geologist. You called me *Kouschka*, little cat. Sometimes I
stopped by the civil-engineering library where you sat with other
foreign students. You were embarrassed; my husband might
catch you. He was in the chemistry lab with his Bunsen burner
boiling water for tea. Alexander Mehielovitch Touritzen, fig of
my pallid college days, plum of my head, did the silk stocking
factory go up in flames? Did the German fox jump out of the
desert's sleeve and gobble your father up? Are you dead?

Second-hand engine, formula concrete, we were still meeting in
stairwells when the best chess player in Champaign-Urbana went
to the Spanish Civil War. He couldn't resist heroic gestures. For
years I was haunted by the woman who smashed her starving
infant against the Spanish wall. Cautious, staid Mehielovitch, so
quick to pick my hairpins out of your bed.
Average lover, have your balls decayed?

Mehielovitch, my husband the chemist with light eyes and big
head, the one whose body I hated, came back in the flesh fifteen
years ago. He was wearing a tight western shirt he had made
himself. (There wasn't anything he couldn't do.) He talked about
wine- and cheese-tasting parties.
We folk-danced at a ski lodge. So this is life, I said.
He told my daughter he was her daddy. It wasn't true.
You are all so boring. My friend from Japan, Cana Maeda, the
scholar of classical haiku, whose fingers, whose entire body had

been trained to comply: her face pale without powder, her neck
so easily bent, after she died from the radiation her translations
of Bashō were published by interested men who failed to print
her correct name. So the narrow book appears to have been
written by a man. Faded in these ways, she is burned on my flesh
as kimonos were burned on the flesh of women in the gamma
rays of Hiroshima. She wasn't one of those whose skin peeled in
the holocaust, whose bones cracked. Graceful and obscure, she
was among all those others who died later. Where are you, my
repulsive White Russian? Are you also lost?

Pimpled obscene boy employed at an early age by your father,
you pandered his merchandise on trays using your arm as a
woman's leg slipped inside a silk stocking with a woman's shoe
on your hand. Do you understand that later I lived with a
transvestite, a hairdresser who wore wigs? When he felt that way
he would go out and pick up an English professor. After we
quarreled, I cut up his foam-rubber falsies. I had a garage sale
while he was out of town. I sold his mail-order high heels, his
corsets, his sequined evening gowns.

Those afternoons in bed listening to your memories of prostitutes
with big breasts, how you wanted to roll on a mattress of
mammary glands; the same when Rip Hanson told me about the
invasion of France. Crossing the channel he saw infantry, falling
past him from split-open cargo planes, still clinging to tanks and
bulldozers. Statistical losses figured in advance. The ripped-open
remnants of a Russian girl nailed up by the Germans outside her
village, also ancient, indigenous.
But what can I tell you about death? Even your sainted mother's soft
        dough body: her flour-dusted breasts
by now are slime paths of microorganisms.
Where were you when they fed the multitudes to the ovens?
Old fetid fisheyes, did they roll you in at the cannery?
Did you build their bridges or blow them up?
Are you burned to powder? Were you mortarized?
Did you die in a ditch, Mehielovitch? Are you exorcised?

Poor innocent lecher, you believed in sin.
I see you rising with the angels, thin forgotten dirty-fingered son
of a silk stocking factory owner in Constantinople,
may you be exonerated. May you be forgiven.
May you be a wax taper in paradise,
Alexander Mehielovitch Touritzen.

Who Is the Widow's Muse?

1991

All Time Is Past Time

Goliath is struck by the stone.
The stone turns into a bird.
The bird sings in her window.
Time is absurd. It flows backward.
It is married to the word.

This is the window of the giant's eyes.
This is the bird singing alone.
This is the river of forgetting.
This is the chosen stone.
This is Goliath's widow.

Struck by the stone he leaps
into the future. He lies
a monolith, a rune, light
from a distant nova. Not even a bone
remembers begetting him ever.

The song is a monotone.
She is the word and the window.
She is the stone and the bird.
She is the bed of the river.

I

Crow, are you the widow's muse?
You wear the weeds.
Her answer, a caw.
Her black beads:
two jet eyes.
A stick fire
and a thorn for her body.
Into the wind, her black shawl.

VI

What is this impatience
the widow says every morning —
Who's here?
Nevertheless,
she brews the coffee,
looks through the cupboards.
Today she won't try to be clever.
Everything has a flat patina
like a dirty window.
The widow's muse is probably
a char woman with a hangover.

VIII

"Am I, then, the widow's muse?"
cries the widow.
"Is alone more alone
than I was led to believe?"
The sexton takes her hand.
He is willing to dig the hole,
he says —
to do the dirty work,
but that's it.
If she wants to have a second coming,
she's going to have to raise it
on her own.

XIII

Alone in the car,
the widow makes songs to him.
She tells him her secrets.
The body of the car holds her;
it is not silent,
it too sings and responds.
She wonders if the muse is the car.
She and the car have
sculptured a comfortable place.
Her feet are at home.
Her hands clasp the steering wheel.
Her eyes seek the way
and the car knows.
Then why has she named the car
Violet Hunt?
The widow sighs. Here it is again—
gender and sorrow.

XVIII

I must be serious, the widow thinks,
I must face reality.
This isn't a temporary separation.
(Perhaps the widow's muse is expectation.)
Actually the widow thinks he may be
in another country in disguise —
that one day he will come back.
He was only fooling.
That was someone else that they buried.

XX

The Widow's Song

As I was a springbok,
I am a leper.
As my skirt lifted up as a veil,
so the shawl of a widow.
As the oxlip,
so the buffalo grass.
As the wall of a garden in winter,
so was I, hidden.
As the game of the keeper...
not counted.
So I am without number.
As the yellow star grass.

XLV

The widow puts on her Long Beach
Literary Women's Festival shirt.
Stained with coffee, it keeps
her company in bed.
That's where we wear our scars
and badges, anyway, she says.
The widow's muse was at the Festival, too.
She was that one with iron gray hair
and the large manila envelope of poems,
who sat next to the widow at dinner.
"Don't read those scary poems," the widow
said. "There are five hundred women here,
and they know all that.
Just get up and give them the old soft shoe."

L

The widow accumulates meaningful trash.
She is no different than all the others.
"I should set aside a room for a shrine.
And how am I going to throw away their little toys?"
She joins the long line of sentimental mothers
waiting for phone calls.
Increasingly, the widow enjoys her grandchildren.
Sometimes she pauses to tell her dead husband...
"It's that time of life when we
should be taking a cruise; going to Europe;
going to Australia. But it's just as well.
The grandchildren need me.
You would have liked them, too."
The muse yawns. The muse is irritable.
"Yes, yes," the muse says;
"So what else is new?"

LII

The widow is told by a great seer
that fifty-two is a magic number.
She consults the muse.
"We must get into a higher gear,"
the muse whispers. "We must shift
out of this phase."
"Just one more about the shoes,"
the widow begs.
The muse shakes her head.
"No. We must get back to the real thing.
The blood and meat of the world."
The muse took the widow in her arms.
"Now say it with me," the muse said.
"Once and for all...he is forever dead."

Simplicity

1995

Look to the Future

To you born into violence,
the wars of the red ant are nothing;
you, in the heart of the eruption.

I am speaking from immeasurable grass blades.
You, there on the rubble,
what is the river of vapor to you?

You who are helpless as small birds
drowned on the ice pack.
You who are spoiled as
commercial fruit by the medfly.

To you the machine guns.
To you the semen of fire,
the birth of the maggot in the corpse.

You, to whom we send these gifts;
at the heart of light we are crushed together.
When the sun dies we will become one.

Plumbing

Plumbing is so intimate.
He hooks up your toilet.
He places a wax ring
under the vitreous seat
where your shit will go.
You are grateful to him.
He is a god with wrenches;
a quiet young man
using a flame torch.
He solders the joints.
He crawls through your dusty attic
over the boxes of doll furniture,
the trains, the ripped
sleeping bags, the Beatles posters,
the camp cots, the dishes, the bed springs,
to wire up the hot water tank.
And you admire him
as you would Saint Francis,
for his simple acceptance
of how things are.
And the water comes like a miracle.
Each time in the night
with your bladder full,
you rise from the bed.
And instead of the awful stench
of the day before and perhaps
even the day before that,
in a moment of pure joy
you smell nothing but the sweet
mold of an old house
and your urine as it sloshes
down with the flush.
And you feel comfortable, taken care of,
like some rich Roman matron
who had just been loved by a boy.

It Follows

If you had a lot of money
(by some coincidence
you're at the Nassau Inn in Princeton
getting a whiff of class)
and you just noticed two days ago
that your face has fallen,
but you don't believe it,
so every time you look in the glass
it's still hanging there where it wasn't.
Would you take the money you needed
for a new roof on your old house
(the house you're paying for
over and over in property taxes)
because it's been leaking for years
and you're tired of emptying buckets
and spraying for mold,
would you take that money
and get your face lifted?
Face-lift. They cut a slit
under your ears and pull up the slack
and they tack it with plastic.
Then they pull up the outer
skin and trim it because it's too long and
fasten that. (Your skin
pulls loose from the fat like chicken skin.)
Because once you were almost
as beautiful as Jane Wyman...
your friends all said that.
Of course at the time she was
married to Ronnie and you were
involved with the ASU—
a McCarthy suspect.
Forget about your neck.
They can't do that yet.
A face-lift lasts five years.

So you could go on being a member
of new-speak and re-entry—
with the unsung benefits
of radiation and by then
your roof would have rotted anyway.
Or been recycled by some corporate kid.
But think how you'd rather
be stripped and streaked
and while you're about it
get some implants of baby teeth buds
that they've taken from dead babies' gums
and frozen for this sort of thing.
You could still die young.

That Winter

In Chicago, near the lake, on the North Shore
your shotgun apartment has a sunroom
where you indulge in a cheap
chaise lounge—
and read *Of Human Bondage*—
There is a window in the living room proper
cracked open so your
Persian cat can go outside.
You are on the first floor and upstairs
a loud-mouthed southern woman,
whose husband is away
all week on business trips,
has brought her maid
up from Georgia
to do the work and take care of the baby.
"Oh lord," the southern woman says,
"he wants it spotless on the weekend—"
The maid, who has
smooth brown skin,
is not allowed to sit on the toilet
but she feeds the kid
and changes the dirty diapers.
She washes the dishes,
she cooks the southern meals,
she irons the sheets for the mahogany bed.
The southern woman shouts
at her in a southern drawl,
"Junie, don't sit on that chair
you'll bust it."
The southern woman is at
loose ends five days
waiting for him to come in.
"It's like a honeymoon,
honey," she says—

"When he grabs me,
whooee."
She invites you up and makes
sure you understand
the fine points of being a white woman.
"I can't let her live
here — not in Chicago.
I made her go out
and get herself a room.
She's seventeen.
She bellered and blubbered.
Now I don't know
what she's trackin' in
from men."
It is winter. The ice
stacks up around
the retaining wall —
the lake slaps over
the park benches,
blocks of ice green with algae.
You are getting your mail secretly at a postal box
because your lover is in the Aleutians.
It's during the war and
your disgusting husband
works at an oil refinery
on the South Side.
Up there in the Aleutians
they are knocking the gold
teeth out of the dead Japanese.
One construction worker
has a skin bag with fifty
gold-filled teeth.
He pours them out at
night in his Quonset hut.
He brags about bashing their faces in.
One day you are fooling
around in a downtown music store

waiting for the war to end.
You let a strange teenage boy
talk you into going
home with him.
He lives alone in a basement behind a
square of buildings.
He shows you his knife collection
and talks obsessively about Raskolnikov — suddenly
your genes want to live
and you pull away
and get out of there.
It is almost dusk.
You run until you find the boulevard
sluggish with the 1943 traffic.
You know by now there
isn't much to live for
except to spite Hitler —
The war is so lurid
that everything else is dull.

For Eight Women

Gender loyalty, alien to the pits and ducts of ourselves;
how to unscrew this pattern?

Now here's another matter: the season of bagworms;
and yet the moths were so random, so azure.

One lives alone out of circumstance until the face
in the multiple mirrors is sour dough, full of its own gas.

The ocean is near, swallowing everything—a little cup
of water moving along the galaxy.

In Morocco my child goes down to the beach toward evening.
She forgets her tormentor, the headmaster's wife.

The ocean takes her, the broth of itself flowing inside her.
She rests with her feet in the scallops of water.

I cannot consider Cana, Alice or Shōkō without Verlaine,
Bashō or Connie Smith.

What is this pattern in the light of bagworms? Nevertheless,
the mornings here are a sweet shock to the blood.

The light as it falls on the louvered windows,
a pattern of slits, and above that, the balconies.

For a short time you are a stranger. Then the vision fades.
Then you become the door, opening and closing.

In the mountains, on my way home from the village, I would
pass my sister's grave. Embalming fluid is pink like antifreeze.

How red she looked in the casket. Next year her grave site caved in.
She stood on her head in the box. The sexton dumped in more dirt.

Dirt, dirty, soil is so useful. We track it in. The white carpet grows
yellow. Down here in the South along highways and boulevards,
    crepe myrtle.

I am a stranger crossing the bone bridge to meet the other.
Our skulls shine like calligraphy in a longed-for language.

Resonance

The universe is sad.
I heard it when Artur Rubinstein played the piano.
He was a little man with small hands.
We were bombing Germany by then.
I went to see him in a dark warehouse
where a piano had been placed for his practice —
or whatever he did before a recital.
He signed the book I had with me —
it was called *Warsaw Ghetto*.
I later heard about him —
his affairs with young women —
if only I had known — but I was
in love with you.
Artur is dead;
and you, my darling,
the imprint of your face, alert like a deer —
oh god, it is eaten away —
the earth has taken it back
but I listen to Artur —
he springs out of the grave —
his genius wired to this tape —
a sad trick of the neural pathways resonating flesh
and my old body remembers the way you touched me.

Things I Say to Myself While Hanging Laundry

If an ant, crossing on the clothesline
from apple tree to apple tree,
would think and think,
it probably could not dream up Albert Einstein.
Or even his sloppy mustache;
or the wrinkled skin bags under his eyes
that puffed out years later,
after he dreamed up that maddening relativity.
Even laundry is three-dimensional.
The ants cross its great fibrous forests
from clothespin to clothespin
carrying the very heart of life in their sacs or mandibles,
the very heart of the universe in their formic acid molecules.
And how refreshing the linens are,
lying in the clean sheets at night
when you seem to be the only one on the mountain,
and your body feels the smooth touch of the bed
like love against your skin;
and the heavy sac of yourself relaxes into its embrace.
When you turn out the light,
you are blind in the dark
as perhaps the ants are blind,
with the same abstract leap out of this limiting dimension.
So that the very curve of light,
as it is pulled in the dimple of space,
is relative to your own blind pathway across the abyss.
And there in the dark is Albert Einstein
with his clever formula that looks like little mandibles
digging tunnels into the earth
and bringing it up, grain by grain,
the crystals of sand exploding
into white-hot radiant turbulence,
smiling at you, his shy bushy smile,
along an imaginary line from here to there.

Metamorphosis

One day you wake up and you have a new face.
What's this? you say
in the harsh kosher manner
of your mother-in-law in a high-class restaurant.

Although your hair is Titian red
and not blue rinse like hers, she always sent whatever it was back—
No matter how many times you look in the mirror
you can't make it go away.

So this is it.
All those women
you thanked God you didn't look like
have surfaced from caves in your cells
where they have been waiting for years
to gather you into their coven.

And now you remember her bitterness;
too much salt, burned edges;
it was never good enough.

The Sperm and the Egg

The sperm hate the egg.
They are afraid of it.
An ogress.
They clot the hot
red anteroom,
clinging to the walls.
She is blue and pulsing.
They are small and inadequate
and lose their tails.
Their chlorine milk begins to spoil.
But on the journey
when the shudder swept them
into an excited knot and
expelled them all together,
early sight scattered ahead of them.
They traveled like a shower of comets.
It was as if they were the universe.

The egg puts out her slimy pseudopod
and takes the sperm into the jelly.
The sperm is hysterical.
Now the egg is busy changing shape.
The sperm does not want to
be pulled apart into strings.
"Don't unravel me," it cries.
The egg does not hear it.
Deep inside the sperm
a seething hatred for the egg.
"When I had my tail,
I was free," the sperm cries.
It remembers the ultimate
vast trajectory.
It remembers them all crying,
"To be or not to be!"

Talking to the Dead

My talk to you, a continuous invention,
like a sailor's tatting;
the casual thread between fingers
becoming medallions.
Far back in the sailor's nebula of neurons,
the delicate spread of lace.

Hooking this word to this word,
my talk with you is slip stitch,
a French-knot;
embroidery over the plain cloth
of waking and sleeping.

Upstairs in the back room,
my unfinished appliqué quilt,
folded away year after year,
with the same last stitch
and the same motionless needle.

My talk with you is not like the redwing
or nuthatch,
not so practical now.
More like the snowmelt
that cannot be stopped.
Cold and liquid,
its crystals shattered,
its pendulous breasts and testicles
rotting together;
the sweat of the snow
without muscle or will,
the plaything of gravity
says what I say to you:
the babble of nothing to nothing.

For My Dead Red-Haired Mother

I loved a red-haired girl.
Freud knew it was a wicked thing to do.
This is how all poems begin.
Sometime after the age of two
I beat the Adam in me black and blue.
Infant, wicked infant!
I threw my love outside
and grew into a bride.

You and I reflecting in our bones
the sea and sky,
we dressed ourselves as flesh,
we learned to lie.

Dearly beloved,
forgive me for that mean and meager self,
that now would mingle
but must first die.

Simplicity

I must retrace my exact steps on the crust,
or I will sink knee-deep in snow.
Kneeling to dip water from the open center of the brook—
between the ridged armies of black trees,
a splinter of light along the line of frost.
Clear as a printed map,
wrinkled skin on a cup of boiled milk—
the mountains of the moon, a full disk edging up.
Dreading all day to come here for this necessary water,
temperature dropping toward zero;
under the ice the water's muscular flow,
its insane syllables, is like a human voice.
Inside the house, sleep, sleep.
I brace myself to lift the weight on either hand.
Picking up my full kettle and bucket
and fitting my feet inside their frozen tracks,
I return under the risen moon,
following my shadow.

Ordinary Words

1999

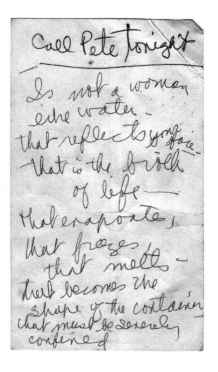

Good Advice

Here is not exactly here
because it passed by there
two seconds ago;
where it will not come back.
Although you adjust to this —
it's nothing, you say,
just the way it is.
How poor we are,
with all this running
through our fingers.
"Here," says the Devil,
"Eat. It's Paradise."

Words

Wallace Stevens says,
"A poet looks at the world
as a man looks at a woman."

I can never know what a man sees
when he looks at a woman.

That is a sealed universe.

On the outside of the bubble
everything is stretched to infinity.

Along the blacktop, trees are bearded as old men,
like rows of nodding gray-bearded mandarins.
Their second-hand beards were spun by female gypsy moths.

All mandarins are trapped in their images.

A poet looks at the world
as a woman looks at a man.

1941

I wore a large brim hat
like the women in the ads.
How thin I was: such skin.
Yes. It was Indianapolis;
a taste of sin.

You had a natural Afro;
no money for a haircut.
We were in the seedy part;
the buildings all run-down;
the record shop, the jazz
impeccable. We moved like
the blind, relying on our touch.
At the corner coffee shop,
after an hour's play, with our
serious game on paper,
the waitress asked us
to move on. It wasn't much.

O mortal love, your bones
were beautiful. I traced them
with my fingers. Now the light
grows less. You were so angular.
The air darkens with steel
and smoke. The cracked world
about to disintegrate,
in the arms of my total happiness.

How They Got Her to Quiet Down

When the ceiling plaster fell in Aunt Mabel's kitchen
out in the country (she carried her water uphill
by bucket, got all her own wood in),
that was seventy-five years ago, before she
took her ax and chopped up the furniture.
Before they sent her to the asylum.
Shafe, father of the boys (she didn't have a girl),
was running around with a loose woman.
Earlier Shafe threw the baby up against the ceiling.
"Just tossing him," he said. Little Ustie came down
with brain fever. In two days that child was dead.
Before that, however, the boys all jumped
on the bed upstairs and roughhoused so
that one night the ceiling fell in;
all lumped on the floor. The kitchen was a sight.
But those kids did not go to the poorhouse.
Grandma was elected to take them.
Mabel's sisters all said, "Ma, you take the boys."
Beauty is as beauty does. Grandma chased them
with a switch until they wore a bare path
around her last cottage. Grandma was small
and toothless, twisted her hair in a tight bun.
After she smashed the furniture, Mabel tried
to burn the house down. Years later when they
let Mabel out of the asylum, she was so light
you could lift her with one hand.
Buddy took her in and she lay on the iron bed
under a pieced quilt. "Quiet as a little bird," he said.

So What

For me the great truths are laced with hysteria.
How many Einsteins can we tolerate?
I leap into the uncertainty principle.
After so many smears you want to wash it off with a laugh.
Ha ha, you say. So what if it's a meltdown?
Last lines to poems I will write immediately.

Madison in the Midsixties

Names, can you talk without their mirage?
What was his name...that rock star,
the one whose plane went down in the lake?
Trees talked all winter in click language.
It was a long drive from the East.
I arrived penniless;
called the Chairman.
"Find a motel," he said.
I could hear the background dinner party.
"Take a motel."
I sat in the Oldsmobile.
The Olds would later drop its front end
on the interstate,
my mother in the backseat
and the hamster and Abigail.
University, where Roger, the graduate student,
gave me his endless poems to read, all
under the influence of Vasco Popa,
all mediocre.
The futile student protests,
napalm and the Feds.
My brains wadded like the Patchwork Girl of Oz;
maced lungs, the National Guard
lined up on either side of the main walk,
rifles cocked just above the passing heads,
a surefire canopy of death.
This montage upon which we write the message
that fails in language after language.

Male Gorillas

At the doughnut shop
twenty-three silver backs
are lined up at the bar,
sitting on the stools.
It's morning coffee and trash day.
The waitress has a heavy feeling face,
considerate with carmine lipstick.
She doesn't brown my fries.
I have to stand at the counter
and insist on my order.
I take my cup of coffee to a small
inoffensive table along the wall.
At the counter the male chorus line
is lined up tight.
I look at their almost identical butts,
their buddy hunched shoulders,
the curve of their ancient spines.
They are methodically browsing
in their own territory.
This data goes into that vast
confused library, the female mind.

Never

Don't forget that Henry James,
because he was afraid
of his hostility toward women
and his sentimental attachment to men,
spread his impotence into language.
He went on and on and couldn't cum.

His style differed from Proust's.
Proust delayed the sensual,
dragging the orgasm out for pages,
until the entire skin of the body
was tortured with pleasure.

But he came, yes, by transvestite
or by tea and cake. The disrobing
went on slowly over and over;
the sensual countryside,
the ridiculous fag, the elegant taster,
the style; coarse broad breast,
kitchen and ballroom, spite
and desperate addiction; climax,
always long drawn-out climax
that only one lying for years
remembering could make
every moment into an hour,
the immortal flesh.

Absence Proves Nothing

By noon I can't stop writing.
I'm on the back of last night,
a reverse gallop.
Last night I lay turning — asking —
what is the telephone pole good for
if not the woodbine?
Because of men, women translate fear.
Thus, all women present subliminally.
That the killer did not come last night
proves nothing.
At night, what is a glass window?
Only a dark space reflecting yourself.
Only a lens for the one outside.

Relatives

Grandma lives in this town;
in fact all over this town.
Grandpa's dead.
Uncle Heery's brain-dead,
and them aunts! Well!
It's grandma you have to contend with.
She's here — she's there!
She works in the fast-food hangout.
She's doing school lunches.
She's the crossing guard at the school corner.
She's the librarian's assistant.
She's part-time in the real-estate office.
She's stuffing envelopes.
She gets up at three a.m.
to go to the screw factory;
and at night she's at the business school
taking a course in computer science.

Now you take this next town.
Grandpa's laid out neat in the cemetery
and grandma's gone wild and bought a bus ticket
to Disneyland.
Uncle Bimbo's been laid up for ten years
and them aunts
are all cashiers in ladies' clothing
and grandma couldn't stand the sight of them
washing their hands and their hair
and their panty hose.
"It's Marine World for me," grandma says.

Then

That summer, from the back porch,
we would hear the storm like a train,
the Doppler effect compressing the air;
the rain, a heavy machine, coming up
from below the orchard, rushing toward us.
My trouble was I could not keep you dead.
You entered even the inanimate,
returning in endless guises.
And that winter an ermine moved into the house.
It was so cold the beams cracked.
The ermine's fur was creamy white
with the last half of the tail soot black.
Its body about ten inches long,
it slipped through small holes.
It watched us from a high shelf in the kitchen.
In our loss we accepted the strange shape of things
as though it had a meaning for us,
as though we moved slowly over the acreage,
as though the ground modulated like water.
The floors and the cupboards slanted to the west,
the house sinking toward the evening side of the sky.
The children and I sitting together waiting,
there on the back porch, the massive engine
of the storm swelling up through the undergrowth,
pounding toward us.

Ordinary Words

Once I called you a dirty — whatever.
Now it does not matter
because your clothes have become
a bundle of rags.
Then I wanted to see what it felt like.
I paid with my life for that.
It went behind your skull.
My middle-class beauty, testing itself,
discovered the dull dregs of ordinary marriage.
Thick lackluster spread between our legs.
We used the poor lovers to death.

Like an ancient reed,
three notes in the early morning,
in the mountains
where I have never traveled,
the blind bird remembers its sorrow.

When

When you return, iron maiden,
jaws of despair,
the thrifty will have eaten the fat.
I, too, have lived on her; the old woman.

When the house is empty,
those outside stare in;
only the flapping door.
Iron maiden, cruel jaws of despair,

when you return, her face will be like that;
the door to the cellar standing open.
When you show your mouth of nails,
only the wind's body will be there.

Residue

Will I ever feel again?
Living at loose ends,
nothing finished.
The odor of your body
sometimes returns
in the afternoon.
A déjà vu rises from
books in the back room,
poems of Wallace Stevens;
your Fruit of the Loom shorts
packed so long in the attic,
alternately freezing and thawing;
or the picture of Delmore Schwartz
sitting on a bench
in a small fenced-in park;
his long gangster-style coat,
his legs crossed;
the edges of a newspaper
lifting in the wind;
his vacant stare, dead white,
vaguely petulant, lost.
Trying to remember you,
I ask myself, who
was that dark Semite?
Your face, your voice,
all but your hands
and feet, faded.

Schmaltz

Those rented rooms,
borrowed beds,
when I would lie down
with my length slack against yours
and feel those simple wounds
of the surfaces
with no thought of the garrote.
And here, after all these years,
I am still thinking
if only one more time,
that ordinary naked touch,
unconscious of its death.
And then, this morning,
the shock of an old song,
after the usual trash of the news;
schmaltz, from the big-band days;
and Sinatra, of course,
on a scratched record,
the local radio's nostalgia.
It is brief, but for a moment
my body shakes
with the remembered tremor
of your voice.
And then, the aftershock:
that he could bring it back —
this grief for which there is no cure.

A Moment

Across the highway a heron stands
in the flooded field. It stands
as if lost in thought, on one leg, careless,
as if the field belongs to herons.
The air is clear and quiet.
Snowmelt on this second fair day.
Mother and daughter,
we sit in the parking lot
with doughnuts and coffee.
We are silent.
For a moment the wall between us
opens to the universe,
then closes.
And you go on saying
you do not want to repeat my life.

In the Next Galaxy

2002

When I am sad
I sing
remembering the red
wing blackbirds
clock –
Then I want no
thing –
except To Turn
time back

For Reservations: 1-800-331-3131

Professor Creeley

This is the end of
March
The tax collector
wants me To cut
my wrists –
the roach inspector
drives up in
a truck →

The Professor Cries

This is the end of March.
The tax collector
wants me to cut my wrists.
The roach inspector
drives up in a truck.
The snow sits like dough
turning sour. Every hour
love's bones grow lighter.
This is what comes
of having no pity.
Time used me.
Death used me.
I live in Johnson City.

Spring Beauties

The abandoned campus,
empty brick buildings and early June
when you came to visit me;
crossing the states midway,
the straggled belts of little roads;
hitchhiking with your portable typewriter.
The campus, an academy of trees,
under which some hand, the wind's I guess,
had scattered the pale light
of thousands of spring beauties,
petals stained with pink veins;
secret, blooming for themselves.
We sat among them.
Your long fingers, thin body,
and long bones of improbable genius;
some scattered gene as Kafka must have had.
Your deep voice, this passing dust of miracles.
That simple that was myself, half conscious,
as though each moment was a page
where words appeared; the bent hammer of the type
struck against the moving ribbon.
The light air, the restless leaves;
the ripple of time warped by our longing.
There, as if we were painted
by some unknown impressionist.

Always Your Shadow

When I remember the cold mornings
when we slept on your side of the sagging bed;
when I remember the cold edge of the curtain
where the light lay still as the marble edge
of the table where the phone wept, the last ring
in another country; that street of cold frost
and row houses, the gas lamps' pulsing light,
hesitant as your last heartbeats when you hung
by a silk cord on the back of a rented door.
This I often rearrange, I don't accept.
But you lived longer than Frédéric Chopin.
And your ancestors could have come from Warsaw.
Back then, I say, you could have died easily as he,
all those frail geniuses died of syphilis or TB.
In this cluttered room, I am listening to Chopin.
When the hurricane presses the ocean,
and the waters divide like the Red Sea,
though split in half, though split again and again,
what is retrieved is cast and taken as an offering.
As this formless slough that breaks apart,
that adheres and breaks, as the rubble of words,
as the metamorphosis of breath.

In the Next Galaxy

Things will be different.
No one will lose their sight,
their hearing, their gallbladder.
It will be all Catskills with brand-
new wrap-around verandas.
The idea of Hitler will not
have vibrated yet.
While back here,
they are still cleaning out
pockets of wrinkled
Nazis hiding in Argentina.
But in the next galaxy,
certain planets will have true
blue skies and drinking water.

Poems

When you come back to me
it will be crow time
and flycatcher time,
with rising spirals of gnats
between the apple trees.
Every weed will be quadrupled,
coarse, welcoming
and spine-tipped.
The crows, their black flapping
bodies, their long calling
toward the mountain;
relatives, like mine,
ambivalent, eye-hooded;
hooting and tearing.
And you will take me in
to your fractal meaningless
babble; the quick of my mouth,
the madness of my tongue.

Wanting

Wanting and dissatisfaction
are the main ingredients
of happiness.
To want is to believe
there is something worth getting.
Whereas getting only shows
how worthless the thing is.
And this is why destruction
is so useful.
It gets rid of what was wanted
and so makes room
for more to be wanted.
How valueless is the orderly.
It cries out for disorder.
And life that thinks it fears death,
spends all of its time
courting death.
To violate beauty
is the essence of sexual desire.
To procreate is the essence of decay.

What We Have

On the mountain
the neighbor's dog, put out in the cold,
comes to my house for the night.
He quivers with gratitude.
His short-haired small stout body
settles near the stove.
He snores.
Out there in the dark, snow falls.
The birch trees are wrapped in their white bandages.
Recently in the surgical theater,
I looked in the mirror at the doctor's hands
as he repaired my ancient frescos.
When I was ten
we lived in a bungalow in Indianapolis.
My sister and brother, my mother and father,
all living then.
We were like rabbits
in the breast fur of a soft lined nest.
I know now we were desperately poor.
But it was spring:
the field, a botanist's mirage of wild flowers.
The house centered between two railroad tracks.
The tracks split at the orchard end of the street
and spread in a dangerous angle down either side.
Long lines of freight for half an hour clicking by;
or a passenger train,
with a small balcony at the end of the last car
where someone always stood and waved to us.
At night the wrenching scream and Doppler whistle
of the two a.m. express.
From my window I could see a fireman stoking
the open fire, the red glow reflected in the black smoke
belching from the boiler.
Once I got up and went outside.
The trees-of-heaven along the track swam in white mist.

The sky arched with sickle pears.
Lilacs had just opened.
I pulled the heavy clusters to my face
and breathed them in,
suffused with a strange excitement
that I think, when looking back, was happiness.

Reality

As a fish, gutted for trade,
so my darling as a cadaver
was slit, his viscera removed;
pulled out by a gloved hand
as waste; the still pulsing
microscopic flagella,
only recently going about its business
in the small scape of the veins,
the glut of the great esophagus
and the first bend of the squirming bowel.
He who was so lovely
with his dark brows and hawk-like nose,
his teeth, irregular from childhood poverty,
or those mobile and compassionate lips
through which he breathed
sweet deadly smoke and words.
The absurd corpse, its now useless testicles
hung below that flaccid thing,
that limp thumb of shriveled skin.
All that sprang up in him so mortal,
so beautiful; come to this.

Sorrow and No Sorrow

We eat through tubes of time
as the cockroach,
as the apple and the codling moth,
as worms of neutrinos;
and what is not there
is always more than there.
As the dropped fawn,
dappled and cinnamon;
as the wind lays the fern aside
and carries the fawn's milk breath
over the ravenous field
on its indifferent tongue.

Train Ride

All things come to an end;
small calves in Arkansas,
the bend of the muddy river.
Do all things come to an end?
No, they go on forever.
They go on forever, the swamp,
the vine-choked cypress, the oaks
rattling last year's leaves,
the thump of the rails, the kite,
the still white stilted heron.
All things come to an end.
The red clay bank, the spread hawk,
the bodies riding this train,
the stalled truck, pale sunlight, the talk;
the talk goes on forever,
the wide dry field of geese,
a man stopped near his porch
to watch. Release, release;
between cold death and a fever,
send what you will, I will listen.
All things come to an end.
No, they go on forever.

The Cabbage

You have rented an apartment.
You come to this enclosure with physical relief,
your heavy body climbing the stairs in the dark,
the hall bulb burned out, the landlord
of Greek extraction and possibly a fatalist.
In the apartment leaning against one wall,
your daughter's painting of a large frilled cabbage
against a dark sky with pinpoints of stars.
The eager vegetable, opening itself
as if to eat the air, or speak in cabbage
language of the meanings within meanings;
while the points of stars hide their massive
violence in the dark upper half of the painting.
You can live with this.

Mantra

When I am sad
I sing, remembering
the redwing blackbird's clack.
Then I want no thing
except to turn time back
to what I had
before love made me sad.

When I forget to weep,
I hear the peeping tree toads
creeping up the bark.
Love lies asleep
and dreams that everything
is in its golden net;
and I am caught there, too,
when I forget.

In the Dark

2004

Like being blind
is synonomous
with being dirty,
yes, one cannot
scrutenizer.
But we're all
blind to the life
on our upper lips-
or the forests in our
mouths-
pink, bizzare folliage,
O, are there horned
lizzards under my tongue?
And what strange
things I think
about-
now that I am blind.

Accepting

Half-blind, it is always twilight.
The dusk of my time and the nights
are so long, and the days of my tribe
flash by, their many-colored cars
choking the air, and I lie like a shah
on my divan in this 21st-century
mosque, indifferent to my folded
flesh that falls in on itself,
almost inert, remembering crossing
the fields, turning corners, coming
home to the lighted windows,
the pedestrian years of it, accepting
from each hand the gifts,
without knowing why they were
given or what to make of them.

Another Feeling

Once you saw a drove of young pigs
crossing the highway. One of them
pulling his body by the front feet,
the hind legs dragging flat.
Without thinking,
you called the Humane Society.
They came with a net and went for him.
They were matter-of-fact, uniformed;
there were two of them,
their truck ominous, with a cage.
He was hiding in the weeds. It was then
you saw his eyes. He understood.
He was trembling.
After they took him, you began to suffer regret.
Years later, you remember his misfit body
scrambling to reach the others.
Even at this moment, your heart
is going too fast; your hands sweat.

An Imprint of the Roaring Twenties

I have a weakness for grubbing at the Salvation Army's discard tables:
old sheets, halves of curtains, soiled pillows,
sometimes a quaint hand-embroidered card table cloth
like the ones my cousin Frances used
when her three young, married, and in-trouble friends
gathered in her bungalow living room
trading their sorrows, their silver liquor flasks,
the stories of their dismal bedroom suites.

Frances served desserts with whipped cream.
Her women friends spent almost every morning in her bungalow,
playing cards and comparing their men.
The ashtrays were emptied and filled again and again.
Two of the women had not yet bobbed their hair.
Just before noon they would gather up the cards
(they gambled for cash)
and spread the starched ironed tablecloth,
like a dead body for viewing. They all helped.
They knew the routine. Frances's tea towels,
exquisite cross-stitched hand-hemmed linen,
hung in her kitchen only for display.
The dingy rags she really wiped her dishes with
were hidden under the sink.

When I was fourteen, and still imprinting like a baby duck,
I went with Frances to visit one of these friends.
She banged the knocker.
We waited a considerable time for an answer.
Finally, the friend barely cracked open the door.
She was wiping her face with her apron.
Her eyes were swollen almost shut,
she was incoherent, her manner distraught.
She didn't invite us in.
We went away, Frances saying, "It's Jim.

He's left her for that slut. She thought
they were just trading partners again."

Like the others, Frances got divorced.
Her husband, Joe, was an alcoholic bookkeeper
in the office of the Norfolk and Western.
So she married a richer, older railroad man,
but he died a few years after
(mean-mouthed relatives said she drove him to it)
and Frances drank herself into senility.

She fell into bouts of paranoia. The family
refused to answer when she knocked.
The nursing home where she was sent
gradually acquired her bungalow and other assets.
I suppose someone got the wicker furniture, the tea towels,
and the card table-size embroidered tablecloths.

Am I

I am outside the Boston Psychopathic.
I ascend to the third floor and look in a window.
Denis Leigh, neurosurgeon and Freudian analyst,
is sitting at his desk. He has my case.
Later in a suburb of London he will say over the phone,
when I tell him my husband has hung himself,
"Well, what do you want me to do about that?"
His wife explains that it is his arthritis
that makes him so irritable.
The suicide had nothing to do with international crisis.
His death came between wars.
He may have identified with Keats (owls, nightingales,
Hampstead Heath), but it was only a rooming house.
The problem with all this is, first I saw the psychiatrist,
then the events. Did he die before or afterward?
However, the doctor played tennis.
The window overlooks the Atlantic. The porthole
is open. The mineral air, so good for you.
Or in the ship's bar, queasy, listening, with the swell,
you smell the spar varnish.
How inadequate; right out of the avenues
of Indianapolis, running in from the outskirts,
you seem to have brought Mr. Vogule along with you.
He was the grade-school janitor from Switzerland
who had a tobacco-yellowed mustache
and danced and sang and slept by the furnace
and shoveled the path through the snow
to the girls' outdoor toilet. See, you say,
that was easy. The doctor knows you are there.
He is making his English effort to be severe with
your attractive body. You are sitting across from him
in the patient's chair. By now he will be seventy or dead.
He gave you bad advice. The usual educated, ignorant,
British male practice. If you looked quickly, you could
see his slight smile go slack. All the time his wife

was secretly calling him from overseas. Someone
wanted him for handball. "Am I crazy?" you asked an intern
late the first night in the sterilized room;
your personality like moth wings, shredding itself
on the hospital furniture. "I don't know," he said.
It was a hard fact.

And So Forth

Someone, or a group of someones,
has gone to consider the strange altered behavior
of penguins along the tip of South America.
It's a film and reporting thing to do.
And someone like me thinks upon it.
Here in darkest Binghamton, I think of the plight of penguins
in the rapidly changing climate
of the oceans and polar regions.
As even now, lightning flashes in mid-December,
and rain and ice coat the glistening asphalt.
This small polluted cluster of towns,
spawned by the shoemaking industry.
Many fat people,
their genes programmed to make fat,
waddle about the streets of these now
mall-dominated towns.
And shoes are made overseas.
The World Wide Web is absolutely nothing,
multiplied by what seems to be an infinite number.
As we swing upon it, filling its no-space
with our so-called communications,
we are filled with the almost perfect vacuum
of nothing at all.
But as an Adélie penguin becomes my own penguin,
inside my skull, even its oil-coated sleek body
that stands and waddles toward its own nest,
somewhere among the million other nests,
and its own chick crying out
among the million others, is distinctive.
Can I hope the great ear of the universe
is pressed to the wall of space and hears me,
its own chick peeping? Over here in this galaxy,
this little freight of penguins
and so forth?

Interim

Like the radiator that sits
in the kitchen passing gas;
like the mop with its head
on the floor, weeping;
or the poinsettia that pretends
its leaves are flowers;
the cheap paint peels
off the steamed walls.
When you have nothing to say,
the sadness of things
speaks for you.

What Is a Poem?

Such slight changes in air pressure,
tongue and palate,
and the difference in teeth.
Transparent words.
Why do I want to say ochre,
or what is green-yellow?
The sisters of those leaves on the ground
still lisp on the branches.
Why do I want to imitate them?

Having come this far
with a handful of alphabet,
I am forced,
with these few blocks,
to invent the universe.

My Mother's Phlox

for Ingrid

To send this to you toward the end of summer,
I was forced to rebuild my desktop.
Not in the old-fashioned way,
with saw and eye laid alongside the board
with some rue in my fingers,
that is, a slight tremble due
to anxiety and missing that former expertise;
but I wanted to create phlox.
Although, god knows, it can't be done
in three dimensions, as the earth
has so easily done it, but who can compete
with the earth? No, I wanted only the words
and they have lost themselves in the fields
or along the gravel road. It's just as well.
(floks) n. pl. various plants of the genus Phlox,
having opposite leaves and flowers,
with variously colored salverform corolla.
Over the years the phlox have spread
even into the fields beyond the barn,
into the edge of the woods, inventions
of themselves in endless designs,
now getting ragged and crepey as
the firm flesh will when it goes on too long.
But what is too long? These phlox
linger at the edges of the lawn. They exhale
their faint perfume summer after summer,
and summer after summer it was my nightlong
intoxicant. It was my potion, my ragged butterfly,
my faulty memory of my mother
who was the same age then, as I am now.
As then, I was the same age you are now,
when my mother planted these phlox in my garden.
I'm sending them to you by UPS,

wrapped in plastic in a proper box.
Take them out and stick them in water;
dig a good bed and spread the roots.
They need almost no care.
They cast their seed; they thrive on neglect.
Later they change like the faces you love,
ravaged and ravishing from year to year.

The Wailing Wall

On and off the air spits a little snow.
This changed water is so beautiful.
I think your bones are also beautiful.
Remote body, trembling with the rush
of traffic; body of altered elements.
You are my beggar's sack, the weight
of this slipping shadow, this eclipse.
You evaporate as these words evaporate.

Crows pump the air across this space;
even they are awkward in the cold.
Their grace disintegrates but not like yours.
Not yet. Another spit of snow. The lines
of chaos, fractal patterns, atmosphere.
This change of shape, this change of entity,
a strangeness like the way I miss your feet,
the way my feet loved your feet in our bed.
The way I have no bed, no resting place.

Negative

My taste of old-fashioned wolf
in wolf's clothing,
a man like all other men
that I never knew;
if I could remember your name,
as the negative fresh from the acid
and into the fixer,
the way I remember the hard
lab table where you pushed me down
and pulled off my skirt.
Or the picnic; your basket
of thin-sliced sandwiches,
and the way you discovered
my breasts weren't nubile;
and I bicycled back
on the powdered road, unfit
to be touched by your hard,
burned hands, the bleached hairs
on your arms; your Princeton
assurance going to rack and ruin
in the cornfields of Illinois.

The Message

How is it that I am so fond of font
and yet say nothing with it?
I ride in a carriage, water buffalo
wander outside, but all I see
is he who sits beside me.
My wit construes the carriage
drawn by hand, whose hand
I do not know and yet
we go on talking, he and I,
his face in the shadow.
Where are we going, whose
rice fields dotted with bending
women, whose terraced hills
lie like a quilt in the long draft
toward sunset, or those birds
lifting through the sky, their voices
rattling as wind rattles the dry
reeds in the marshes.
I am aware and yet I am asleep.
What he is saying is clear as type,
set by hand and bound for printing.
And yet it is upside down and backward.
I press it to my body and read it
through my skin. It is the primer
of our ancestors. It says nothing
is sacred, nothing repeats.

What Love Comes To: New & Selected Poems

2008

At night you look at me
from your ivory sockets,
as if this mistake had
never been made.
As if the ferrel blood
still served.
A body laid out
on a rusty scuttle,
in a brittle cage,
you probe like a white rat
looking for openings;
the buzzer,
your dismembered extasy.

Imprint of the Stereoscopic Cards

If you make a connection between this table and that table,
then you will remember your grandmother's loaves of bread
and from there you arrive outside the gates of Jerusalem.
Your jealous and unkind aunt Virginia, who is six years older
than you, has made it a rule that you must look at each card,
even that one of the lepers. Your grandmother knows nothing of this.
Rotting in rags, their voices crying, "Unclean, unclean."
The lepers' lips are eaten away. They hold out their stumps.
Bones come through their soiled wrappings.
And yet they are odorless on the stereoscopic cards.

Bread is made twice a week on the scrubbed kitchen table.
You are seven, waiting for the boxed tour of Jerusalem.
The trick of two eyes and two photographs.
Then your whole body enters into that place.
You take in your mouth the warm buttered bread
from your grandmother's white floured hands.
You sit with the viewer; waiting to slide into focus
the lettered and numbered cards and to hold
for the rest of your life these cast-out bodies of lepers.

All in Time

I

With something to do,
no wonder I sit at the typewriter.
Behind me, the clock has the
monotonous voice of a parent.
Always it is something else I prefer.
The dictionary is a moving finger,
the compressed words of my life.
It's ridiculous, asparagus, asphodel,
accoutrements,
spine in alphabetical order.
More Pope than Pope,
also born hunchback
with a niggling spirit
it sends me a telegram saying,
"If you're close in Melrose, look me up.
You can find me under lexicon."

II

In the West End we could take a cab,
a cob, a Cadillac.
I run into town to send a hot wire
back up the mountain.
No category here by that name.
Suggest you try some party in Cincinnati,
Cryptos, Crimea.

III

Do you take my place,
electron microscope?
Strip of film, blast off,
jet-lagged, space probed,
plastic velvet-lined motor,
sensor cube, in webby

hemispheres;
left right crossing the electric orb,
the bridge of sighs
from my winter to yours;
whispering, shrinking,
blank phonemes fading,
falling.

IV

The cement driller bends down
into the cavity of the street.
Gray gum of the sidewalk sprays from his drill.
Bombarded every day by neutrinos,
I walk down Longest Avenue holding my umbrella.
Information, merely information;
everywhere bone sparkle,
radials sifting deeper into ooze.
How I am coming apart.
How I scatter.
The air sparkles with my dust.

V

Little potato, dried Russian apple,
sweet-cheeked mama
with the singing broom,
I am not even good wine.
You've wasted your vats on me.
Flying snow queen in your wicker carriage
riding over the moon
and farther in those fairy tales,
when the clear morning star sailed in my bedroom window.
We were all barking
and the yellow jackets stung our bare feet
in the deep clover.
Lamps, like those lamps in the evening parlor,
come and go in second-hand shops.
Even the panorama photographs of

between the wars,
and no one laughs that way anymore.

VI

My unknown, my own skeleton,
you will take me where the cartilage loosens
and the blood dries
and I will let go
my burning suns.
I am not Helen,
I die with Carthage.
I see carnage in man.
I dissolve in your old useless salts.
Love and fear attracted my double helix,
broke bonds with me.
Neither man nor woman,
but I remain until then
your singular subject.

VII

Violent creatures of your island continent,
scattered, expelled by the giant
hunting you down,
we ride with our leaping kangaroo.

We are your embryos in the pouch of fire.
We hang out the windows of your brothy sack,
riding with you in the bushfire
under your ribs,
as we swing along the track of naked bullets.

VIII

The rattan lampshade sags
above the incense burner;
the cheap Victorian clock unwinds
like forgotten guilt;

ivy climbs the windows.
Here the embarrassing body,
wrapped in acrylic,
coaxes its thickened veins
and blood gathers in its bulging heart.

IX

I sort my reflections by their titillations,
a little pain, a little physical duress,
a teasing corner of oblivion.
My body, in the multiple stress of the moment,
ages and cracks.
The centipedes confess to finally forgetting which end was first.
The primal fire expands into the inner bubble
of the universe.

Sir William Herschel saw pinpoints
of another kind of space
from which the milk of galaxies was poured,
as from a pitcher.
What is this universe that occupies my face?
I travel in an orderly erratic place.
I am a particle,
I am going toward something. I am complicated,
and yet, how simple is my verse.

X

The top of the poplar is shaking out money,
but it will not fall.
As I am my own sister, it will fall;
as the sun has its humors, it will fall.
But now it tickles itself crying "poor, poor."
Light, controlling birds, dancing midges of light —
history never relents
spending and being spent.
Make heads and tails of this —
poets never make money.

XI

This language, given me from birth,
was not my language.
But in you, I knew a generous woman's voice.
You were puzzled, as I,
at the choices of death,
that we die at birth,
that we die as we are born,
denying ourselves and women.
Even you,
though you secretly gave me one eye which saw,
and one ear which heard.

XII

My father, as you had a shot at her,
you had a shot at me.
My father, as I am your child,
I am the diseased prostitute.
The vessel apart from you;
the container.
As the choir of undescended boys sings of God, the father,
so I sing of my mother —
as the apostles, as the defiled.
Out of this, we come in the endless sadness of children.

Speaking to My Dead Mother

At two a.m. in Binghamton, it's quiet.
I did not comfort you with one last kiss.
Your death was my death. Instinct ran riot.
I ran. Didn't hold your hand at the abyss.
My life had gone like grass fire; like the trees
in drought, caught in the burning wind. And June
returns, another cycled year. Sweet-peas,
dahlias, phlox; the orchard I can't prune;
your small garden gloves, remnants of crystal
stemware. It wears away. I cannot bar
the passage. Jewelweed shoots its pistol
pouch of seeds and the storm, like a guitar,
thrums over the mountain. All that brooded,
ignorant in your safe arms, concluded.

The Dog

The dog is God.
It knows it is God.
It is God living with God.
Even in the rain,
the esters, the pheromones,
calligraphy of the sacred,
the great head points into the wind,
the blood thrashes in the thick veins.
The language of the feces, urine,
species, rut, offal, decay —
nothing is hidden from the dog,
who keeps its own counsel,
leading you by the leash.

Why I Left California

Mildred's mother gave me an umbrella for Christmas.
That was about all I got.
Of course, I wasn't one of the family,
and Mildred was paying the rent.
The rich find it hard to tolerate too much of that.
I couldn't find a job.
The umbrella was see-through plastic with green dots,
but in Sierra Beach it never seemed to rain.

Mildred's mother was about eighty
and she had a widow's hump,
a lump of fat between her shoulder blades.
Her dresses had to be altered
to fit this little fat on her back.
Mildred offered me her mother's retired clothes,
which were from the best California shops.
Shantung or raw silk,
always carefully pressed and just back from the cleaners.
They looked good on the hanger,
but my New England bones
couldn't accommodate that widow's hump.

Mildred asked me to come out and live with her
because she wasn't well.
She kept getting tooth infections,
pneumonia and other things.
For years she had been a sophisticated,
adolescent, Shirley Temple-type beauty,
a young Madame Alexander real living doll.
She was a working writer,
she reported for big-time New York magazines,
like *Esquire.*
She was pumped full of brains and estrogen.
She never grew any older physically.
She was Peter Pan in drag.

But then, her teeth began to give her trouble,
and she got involved with a big-time dentist.
Whatever she did,
Mildred always got involved with the head honcho.
On the set of a movie she was covering,
she would get involved with the director.
Her flirtation with the dentist had ended
and he gave her a nagging bill.
Her love affair, in the dentist chair,
developed a dry socket.
It was getting toward winter,
her jobs had slacked off,
and she suddenly wanted to go back to her origins.
San Loze, California, a zippy small town of grand houses
and swimming pools, the country clubs and lawyers
who were friends of the family
and vice presidents with stocks in old organizations,
like canned milk.
Not movies, but real society and the Yacht Club.
But then she ended up in Sierra Beach
because her sister lived on an island nearby,
and she basically hated her sister,
which made her sister a substitute
for the aching tooth.
Mildred always needed something to harangue about.
The night the earthquake knocked my bed around the room,
there was an eclipse.
I stayed up to watch Earth's shadow.
A blot of black spilling slowly across the moon.
I lay on a lounge out on the patio
and looked at the dark shadow of Earth crossing the sky
like a prehistoric bird swallowing the full disk.
The air was heavy with jasmine and roses
and I knew those bird-of-paradise flowers were out there
with their scarlet beak blossoms.
All that afternoon I had lain back watching the passing monarch butterflies,
in flocks quite big and migrating.

In the anticlimax following the eclipse,
I could finally see again
the silver of the moon on the water,
flickering far down the hill,
the water of the Pacific
in the clasped arms of the lagoon,
the semicircle of sand and gardens that were slowly being eaten away
by the surf and tides.
The house Mildred was renting was at the top of the hill,
overlooking the town of Sierra Beach.
Sometimes the yellow pollution thickened the air
and lay out on the Pacific like rolled-up batting,
ready to come in with the tide
and spread its acid throat-burning smog.
Then Mildred and I would close the doors and windows
and turn on the fans.
But the night of the eclipse was clear.
One of my jobs was to keep the fire going.
Mildred thought that the small iron stove leaked gas,
but here it was necessary on chilly damp days.
The wood was sort of brush,
stacked in the narrow slit between our fence and the house.
I squeezed into this lichen-slick niche and gathered the wood.
There was a continuous dialogue
between Mildred and the owner of the house
about whether the long metal pipe
that rose to the high ceiling
and then fit into a ceramic chimney on the roof
leaked gas.
I was used to wood-burning stoves.
I had one back in Vermont.
I felt Mildred's fears were ridiculous.
But she had an almost masculine side to her.
It would emerge in the voice of authority
and sometimes several tones deeper than her Shirley Temple voice.
Anyway, no smoke leaked out,
but Mildred was prone to engaging in vendettas.

The earthquake merged like cinema into the eclipse.
It was all part of the celluloid dream,
the early morning; still asleep,
I heard the rocks grind under the house.
My bed danced around the room.
It was my first earthquake
but I recognized it instantly.
There were equally strong aftershocks all day long.
The quake seemed like a novelty at first,
but that was my shock.
As the day wore on,
fear and reality became one.
I felt terror.
Buildings had collapsed on top of people.
Overpasses came down on cars.
People who live in California are used to this.
They clean it up and get on.
But after a few days,
I thought I would go back home.
The smog was dark. I was still nervous.
The place felt like an eggshell.
The foundations of the house had shaken apart.
The big rocks were all askew.
I got my bus ticket and packed my few things.
Mildred had instantly invited Woo to come and stay with her.
Woo drove me to the bus station.
The Santa Ana was blowing.

In the mountains, we ran into a snowstorm
that the bus driver couldn't handle,
but I felt right at home.
Although we had to stop over for one night
in a dreary roadside bus station,
I amused myself listening
to the passengers' sad stories.
Greyhound brings out the worst in everyone.
Nevertheless, I remained basically euphoric.

There were no snowplows,
but the snow melted, and we went on through Arizona.
On and on, turning toward New England,
I was happily pointed toward Eastern winter
and the simple hazards of icy roads and frostbite.
I was going home to the creosote and leaking gas
in my own stovepipes and my own woodpile.
Carefully taking with me my plastic umbrella.

The Porch

Whatsoever comes to the screen,
firefly or moth,
I lean back in the wicker chair,
the porch my fragile skin
between me
and the gorgeous open maw,
the sucking swallowing world.

Fragrance

Edna St. Vincent Millay—
her friends called her Vincent—
lived for a time in New York,
in the Village.
E.E. Cummings lived there too—
and even I was living then—
but in the Midwest
in Indianapolis.

Then, my father,
sitting at his Linotype machine,
the hot lead slugs
clicking and falling,
would sometimes print
a poem of mine—
something he found
around the house.

Poems came to me
as if from far away.
I would feel them coming.
I would rush into the house,
looking for paper and pencil.
It had to be quick,
for they passed through me
and were gone forever.
What are children's poems?
Like the sudden breeze
that pulls the petals
from the honeysuckle.

Much later,
when I lived in the Village,
E.E. Cummings was a faint legend.
Poets come and go,

like squills that bloom
in the melting snow.

The Möbius Strip of Grief

When I went into the room where you waited,
you said you were not staying here with me.
Angry, I went back to get an ice pick
where a large block of ice lay on the stairs.
It froze my fingers when I tried to lift it.
I am not a murderer, even in the brilliance
of sleep where poems are three-dimensional.
How often you come this way
in your cold contempt for my ignorance.

Weapons

My student's father
embezzled the company,
his own,
and traveled. Went
to Swaziland,
collected weapons.
She herself laughs
hysterically, is
obsessive about
which university
to try next.
Her parents live
in the same house,
and while he was in
Mongolia on one of his
impulsive trips
she and her mother
hid her father's
gun collection,
some ninety or so
exotic weapons,
in her mother's aunt's
basement.
Still, the student
who returned from three
semesters in Germany,
to take creative writing here
on an impulse,
feels that next year
she would like to expand,
go to work with the best writers,
although she has only
been into poetry
for the last six months.
She can still get financial backing

so she is submitting
ten or eleven poems,
surreal and wrenched
from her unconscious.
And what do I know
about creative writing?
This rapidly mutating world
appears and disappears
like the astrophysicists'
description of subatomic
particles blinking in
and out of the fabric
of space and time.
Who am I to say, words,
words, those tiny
worms of sound,
those strange firing puffs
of disintegrating flesh;
this sack of
self-propelling flesh that
for ninety-one years
has been calling itself me.

Poetry

The sentence is basically a story.
Even a few words attach to the lifetime.
The mouth cannot forget
the story of the fingers.

Like comb jelly,
like canned condensed air,
like the full sac of the cobra;
the bitter milk of the tongue.

Bus Station

The toilets ooze like suppurating sores.
The resident homeless talks to herself.
Wearing all her worldly goods in layers;
her voice comes out of that cocoon.
She sits on tile floor against the damp wall,
holding two bulging trash bags.
She is having an animated conversation
with the empty room. Something angers
her. She argues. Then her head droops.
She dozes. She dozes as I do at night
in my bed, with the lamp in my eyes,
the phone on the bedside table, my glass
of water, aspirin, chocolate mints, emergency
numbers. As I do, snugged in my warm
blankets; a book, let's say, *The Best American*
whatever, slipping between my fingers.

Goshen

For fifteen years I have lived in a house
without running water or furnace.
In and out the front door
with my buckets and armloads of wood.
This is the mountain.
This is the fortress of ice.
This is the stray cat skulking in the barn.
This is the barn with vacant windows
that lifts like a thin balsa kite
in the northeasters.
These are the winter birds
that wait in the bushes.
This is my measuring rod.
This is why I get up in the morning.
This is how I know where I am going.

One Year I Lived in Earlysville, Virginia

In an old farmhouse in the middle of poor pastureland
I came to know the suffering of beef cattle. I was
teaching at the University of Virginia at Charlottesville,
taking the place of a poet who had gone to New York
for the year. The house was also the poet's and I lived
with his cats and his furniture and his books and his
sorrow. Sorrow was everywhere. The fat woodchuck
who lived under the back shed would sit at sundown
on her front stoop with her short arms folded almost
over her stomach and enjoy a rest from digging new
runways or eating the sparse grasses. And over on the
next parcel, the hound dogs would lift their crass
voices, yearning to track her down. For a while a
student shared the house with me. A strange
enterprising young woman who told me how she wrote
her term papers by going into the library and looking up
old thesis manuscripts and copying them. It was
ingenious and probably took more work than writing an
original. But she loved the power of taking what was
not hers. She also won an important poetry prize by
using her friend's letters, chopping the paragraphs into
likely sections. The last I heard of her she was waiting
tables somewhere. Her sadness was like the sadness
of second-hand automobile salesmen.
Near the house, beyond the black walnut trees, an old
family graveyard, surrounded by a quartz-stone wall
and mostly filled with women, children, and many
unnamed babies. The student also haunted second-
hand shops and I went with her once because I
needed a coat. I had discovered Virginia was in the
temperate zone. I was sitting at the desk on the second
floor under the tin roof, where when it rained, as it often
did in the afternoon, the noise was deafening, the
lightning striking the ground with an immense bolt of
zigzag blue. And the second-hand coat was hanging

downstairs on a hook beside the front door. I had recently looked at some old-fashioned postcards. The early twenties, I think, and scenes of some hotel with ladies in dresses that were just beginning to reach their lower calves; ladies who probably still kept their handkerchiefs in boxes and their gloves in bureau drawers. And here I was, living in someone else's life, grieving for the half-starved cattle and the young castrated bulls who would lose the herd and cry out in their terrible lost-mother voices. The coat was a rebuke and not at all a coat that I would have normally worn. I wore blue jeans most of the time and sweaters. But the university was old and mostly male and I was only a visitor so I tried to dress in an acceptable way. The coat created the poem. But I expect some of my Edwardian grandmother got in it. Those endless closets and halls in the brain where the unknown hides; that open for a moment and then close again. That is where the poems come from.

Index of Titles

About the Author

Ruth Stone is an American poet and author of more than thirteen books of poetry. She was born in Roanoke, Virginia, in 1915 and attended the University of Illinois at Urbana-Champaign. For much of her life she resided in Goshen, Vermont, traveling to teach at various universities across the country and finally receiving tenure at SUNY Binghamton. She had a dedicated following for many years and found widespread recognition in her later life. She received many honors, including the 2002 National Book Award for Poetry, the 2002 Wallace Stevens Award, the National Book Critics Circle Award, the Eric Mathieu King Award from the Academy of American Poets, a Whiting Award, two Guggenheim Fellowships, the Delmore Schwartz Memorial Poetry Award, the Walter Cerf Medal for lifetime achievement from the state of Vermont, and the Shelley Memorial Award. The last book she published while living, *What Love Comes To: New and Selected Poems* (Copper Canyon Press), was a finalist for the 2009 Pulitzer Prize for Poetry. She was poet laureate of Vermont from 2007 until her death in November of 2011.

About the Editor

Bianca Stone is a poet and visual artist. Her poems have appeared in *The New Yorker, jubilat,* and *Poetry.* Her newest volume is *A Little Called Pauline,* a children's book of the Gertrude Stein poem. She lives in Vermont.

Poetry is vital to language and living. Since 1972, Copper Canyon Press has published extraordinary poetry from around the world to engage the imaginations and intellects of readers, writers, booksellers, librarians, teachers, students, and donors.

WE ARE GRATEFUL FOR THE MAJOR SUPPORT PROVIDED BY:

THE PAUL G. ALLEN
FAMILY FOUNDATION

CULTURE

Lannan

OFFICE OF ARTS & CULTURE
SEATTLE

WASHINGTON STATE
ARTS COMMISSION

TO LEARN MORE ABOUT UNDERWRITING
COPPER CANYON PRESS TITLES,
PLEASE CALL 360-385-4925 EXT. 103

WE ARE GRATEFUL FOR THE MAJOR SUPPORT PROVIDED BY:

Anonymous

Jill Baker and Jeffrey Bishop

Anne and Geoffrey Barker

Donna and Matthew Bellew

Will Blythe

John Branch

Diana Broze

John R. Cahill

The Beatrice R. and Joseph A.
Coleman Foundation

The Currie Family Fund

Laurie and Oskar Eustis

Austin Evans

Saramel Evans

Mimi Gardner Gates

Linda Fay Gerrard

Gull Industries Inc. on behalf of
William True

The Trust of Warren A. Gummow

Carolyn and Robert Hedin

Bruce Kahn

Phil Kovacevich and Eric Wechsler

Lakeside Industries Inc. on behalf
of Jeanne Marie Lee

Maureen Lee and Mark Busto

Peter Lewis and Johnna Turiano

Ellie Mathews and Carl Youngmann
as The North Press

Hank and Liesel Meijer

Jack Nicholson

Gregg Orr

Petunia Charitable Fund and
adviser Elizabeth Hebert

Gay Phinny

Suzanne Rapp and Mark Hamilton

Adam and Lynn Rauch

Emily and Dan Raymond

Jill and Bill Ruckelshaus

Cynthia Sears

Kim and Jeff Seely

Joan F. Woods

Barbara and Charles Wright

Caleb Young as C. Young Creative

The dedicated interns and
faithful volunteers of
Copper Canyon Press

The Chinese character for poetry is made up of two parts:
"word" and "temple." It also serves as pressmark for
Copper Canyon Press.

The poems are set in Hightower.
Book design and composition by Phil Kovacevich.